READING
ESTHER

LITERARY CURRENTS IN BIBLICAL INTERPRETATION

READING ESTHER

---

a case for the literary carnivalesque

KENNETH M. CRAIG, JR.

•

WESTMINSTER JOHN KNOX PRESS
Louisville, Kentucky

READING ESTHER:
A CASE FOR THE LITERARY CARNIVALESQUE

© 1995 Kenneth M. Craig, Jr.

First edition

Published by Westminster John Knox Press,
Louisville, Kentucky

This book is printed on acid-free paper that meets the American National Standards Institute Z39.48 standard. ∞

PRINTED IN THE UNITED STATES OF AMERICA
2 4 6 8 9 7 5 3 1

Library of Congress Cataloging-in-Publication Data

Craig, Kenneth M., 1960–.
   Reading Esther : a case for the literary carnivalesque / Kenneth M. Craig, Jr.
      p.   c . — (Literary currents in biblical interpretation)
   Includes bibliographical references and indexes.
   ISBN 0-664-25518-3 (pbk. : alk. paper)

   1. Bible. O.T. Esther—Criticism, interpretation, etc. 2. Bible. O.T. as literature.   3. Bakhtin, M. M. (Mikhail Mikhailovich), 1895–1975.   4. Carnival in Literature.   I. Title.   II. Series.
BS1375.2.C73   1995
222′.9066—dc20   95-7833

To my Mother and my Father

CONTENTS

SERIES PREFACE

New currents in biblical interpretation are emerging. Questions about origins—authors, intentions, settings—and stages of composition are giving way to questions about the literary qualities of the Bible, the play of its language, the coherence of its final form, and the relations between text and readers.

Such literary criticism is rapidly acquiring sophistication as it learns from major developments in secular critical theory, especially in understanding the instability of language and the key role of readers in the production of meaning. Biblical critics are being called to recognize that a plurality of readings is an inevitable and legitimate consequence of the interpretive process. By the same token, interpreters are being challenged to take responsibility for the theological, social, and ethical implications of their readings.

Biblical interpretation is changing on the practical as well as the theoretical level. More readers, both inside and outside the academic guild, are discovering that the Bible in literary perspective can powerfully engage people's lives. Communities of faith where the Bible is foundational may find that literary criticism can make the Scripture accessible in a way that historical criticism seems unable to do.

Within these changes lie exciting opportunities for all who seek contemporary meaning in the ancient texts. The goal of the series is to encourage such change and such search, to breach the confines of traditional biblical criticism, and to open channels for new currents of interpretation.

—THE EDITORS

PREFACE

I wish to express my gratitude to a number of persons who have made valuable contributions to my work. My thanks go first to Danna Nolan Fewell and David Gunn for accepting my proposal and for their help throughout this project. I am grateful to members of the Research and Scholarship Committee of the American Academy of Religion for offering me a Research Assistance Grant. G. Kenneth Wolfskill made many helpful comments on my manuscript, and Andrea E. Eason was always helpful when I asked questions about the computer. I read portions of chapter 3 in the "Semiotics and Exegesis Section" at the 1993 national SBL meeting in Washington, D.C. Tina Pippin provided a useful critique in her formal response to my paper. I owe more thanks to my wife, Niki, than to any already mentioned. I have benefited greatly from her support and knowledge. My children, Alexandra and Luke, put the writing in proper perspective, and it is with love and respect that I dedicate this book to my parents, Ken and Janette Craig.

—KENNETH M. CRAIG, JR.

1

INTRODUCTION

There is neither a first nor a last word and there are no limits
to the dialogic context.
> —Mikhail Bakhtin, "Toward a Methodology
> for the Human Sciences"

The house of fiction has not one window but a million.
> —Henry James, *The Art of the Novel*

Mikhail Mikhailovich Bakhtin. The name is spoken today in
virtually every academic corridor, but twenty years ago only
a few Slavic specialists had heard it. Perhaps no twentieth-
century Russian scholar has generated such a profound discourse so far beyond the Soviet borders as Mikhail Bakhtin. The
praise of two critics is not uncommon: "Mixail Baxtin is today
one of the most popular, if not the most popular, figures in the
domain of humanistic studies" (Pomorska 1978:379). "What all
the recent activity in Bakhtin studies suggests is that this very
important thinker—or interlocutor—may finally claim the central
position he deserves as one of the key writers of the century"
(Jackson 1987:420). A survey of books, articles, and reviews
leaves little doubt that the Bakhtin boon may very well be
among the most extraordinary events of recent international
and intellectual history.

The explosion of interest implied by these inflated terms of
praise might suggest that Bakhtin is emerging as a hero-figure as
well as an exceptional thinker in the humanities and the world
of letters. Part of the excitement is due no doubt to the fact that
most of his writings were kept from the public from the 1920s to
the 1970s. The details surrounding many of the events of his life
have only recently become available to Western readers, and,

whatever reservations scholars might have about Bakhtin's different ideas, it is difficult to imagine how anyone could contemplate his life without feeling respect for his accomplishments. Consider, for example, John Sturrock's account:

> In 1929 [Bakhtin] was arrested, and sentenced to six years' exile in Kazakhstan. . . . He survived the harshness of Kazakhstan because he was a simple enough soul to live adequately anywhere. He had no idea of home comforts or of ordinary practicality—he never found out how to use a telephone. His health was bad—but sitting down suited him. What he needed was a desk to write at, a great deal of tea to drink and a great many cigarettes to smoke. A sad little story . . . is [told] of Bakhtin in wartime Moscow slowly rolling the manuscript of a book by him on Goethe into cigarette papers and puffing his way through the entire draft, starting at the end. It was his only manuscript (1986:13).

Bakhtin has generated a powerful discourse about language and literature, despite a crippling bone disease, personal hardship, neglect, and the iron fist of the Soviet machinery that attempted to quash the voices of the Russian intelligentsia. His achievements are as much a global accomplishment as a personal and private triumph of the human spirit.

This study of the Hebrew version of the Esther narrative poses two questions: Should the biblical story of Esther be included with other non-biblical stories generally designated as the literary carnivalesque? On what grounds does insight gleaned from a twentieth-century thinker shed light on an ancient book? Primary attention will be given to the Esther tale as we move back and forth from Bakhtin's writings to the contours of the biblical literary text.[1] The Hebrew tale of Esther, so often categorized as unique (and, for some, disturbingly so) among the books of the Bible, requires special study in the light of popular festive forms or what Bakhtin calls the "carnivalization of literature" (1984a:122). Bakhtin helps us discover, or, as I shall argue in chapter 6, rediscover, a peculiar logic to the images of this "unique" story. My reasons for drawing insight from a twentieth-century thinker in this study of an ancient text will, I hope, soon become apparent. Bakhtin's sense of historical consciousness makes his ideas compelling and enduring. Interpreters often make the observation that the Hebrew version of the Esther tale is overtly non-religious in its language—especially when compared to the Greek versions or to other books of the Hebrew Bible. *Why* this might be the case, however, has not been addressed.[2]

There are many sources of Bakhtin's intellectual energy, and his encyclopedic command of history might remind some readers of Auerbach's classic work, *Mimesis*. Like Auerbach, Bakhtin is a master comparatist. The Russian theoretician drew from ancient grammarians and rhetoricians, and he was as familiar with Hellenistic romances and medieval *fabliaux* as with classic works from the Baroque and Enlightenment eras. His knowledge of Greek and Latin is evident on many of the pages of his oeuvre. He moves from Ion of Chios and Macrobius to a host of eighteenth and nineteenth-century writers of Russia, England, France, and Germany.

It is this sweep of history that explains in part Bakhtin's appeal to those who study culture, language, and communication, to those who are concerned with theories of the novel and poetics, and to researchers who examine philosophical or psychological aspects of human consciousness. Yet while he appeals to literary critics, sociologists, anthropologists, and historians, he remains virtually unnoticed among students of the Bible. Robert Polzin draws insight from Bakhtin on several occasions in *Samuel and the Deuteronomist* (1989),[3] and his article, "Dialogic Imagination in the Book of Deuteronomy" (1984), makes present-day applications of Bakhtin's theories. But these studies by a prominent biblical scholar stand out because they exist in a virtual vacuum.[4]

The place Bakhtin has earned in the humanities might suggest that his insight into the theory of literature is an important tool for students of the Bible, which is, after all, a literary and social document. In this study, I seek to follow a path that Bakhtin has charted, and I wish to suggest that he provides a valuable window, to borrow James's image, for looking at the story of Esther.

BAKHTIN'S MAJOR WORKS
AND THE BAKHTIN CIRCLE

Very little was known of Bakhtin's personal life before the team of Katerina Clark and Michael Holquist conducted research in obscure Russian archives and interviewed a number of Bakhtin's associates. Their biography, *Mikhail Bakhtin*, is an important work and a fascinating story in its own right. One question that invariably arises from their study of his life and work is that of authorship. In a chapter titled, "The Disputed Texts," Clark and Holquist (1984:146-170) discuss the problem of authorship and creativity associated with the name of Bakhtin. Bakhtin published only a few works under his name: a volume on Dostoevsky's poetics (an awkward English translation appeared in 1973, then an expanded and much improved translation in 1984), a book on Rabelais (first published in English in 1968), and several essays. In addition to these writings, he is also sometimes credited as author of other books. *The Formal Method in Literary Scholarship* (1928) was published under the name of Pavel N. Medvedev, a critic who disappeared in the purges of the 1930s. Two other titles, *Freudianism* (1927) and *Marxism and the Philosophy of Language* (1929), were both signed by Valentin N. Voloshinov who died of tuberculosis in 1936.[5]

This is not the place to try to solve the puzzle of Bakhtin's textology, but a few comments about these texts and the treatment of this source material for the present study are in order. Medvedev and Voloshinov along with a half dozen other people[6] form what is generally called today the Bakhtin circle. While the extent of these connections is an open-ended issue, few doubt that there was a network of working relations worthy of the name "circle." The Soviet literary executor of Bakhtin's estate signed a document just before Bakhtin's death indicating that, while two members of the circle, Medvedev and Voloshinov, made some changes or additions to the books that bear their names, these works were, in fact, written by Bakhtin. The document has never been made public, and the executor has made remarks on subsequent occasions that qualify his earlier statement (Medvedev/Bakhtin 1978:ix-xi, xiv, xxvi). A number of scholars have assumed in recent years that Bakhtin was *at*

14

most the co-author of each of the three books in question, but Clark and Holquist argue that virtually everything in these texts comes from Bakhtin's pen. In his essay on Bakhtin, "The Politics of Representation," Holquist presents historical evidence to support this claim (Greenblatt 1981). Todorov, on the other hand, takes the position that the style reflected in these works diverges from that in the undisputed Bakhtin texts. According to Todorov, the texts associated with Medvedev and Voloshinov share a didacticism that is entirely absent from the works published under the name of Bakhtin (Todorov 1981:17-22).

The full extent of Bakhtin's authorship or influence in these disputed texts is unclear, and the issue of his role in composition remains an open question. The range of possibilities is suggested by Clark and Holquist, who accept them almost entirely as the work of Bakhtin, and Todorov, who is more circumspect. The authorial responsibility borne by Medvedev and Voloshinov for the texts that appeared under their names and the lack of direct evidence or testimony that would weigh against such a claim may cause one to raise questions about Clark and Holquist's conclusion. With Todorov, I use the name Bakhtin in this study as a collective designation for the author *and* members of the circle, and work from the assumption that Bakhtin was "the philosopher" of the circle who supplied the intellectual inspiration for the group. Bakhtin's *Rabelais and His World* will serve a foundational role in this study, and other works sometimes attributed to members of the circle will be cited on occasion.

In addition to deciding which texts are actually Bakhtin's, one has also to deal with the problem of his enigmatic writing style. One reviewer refers to Bakhtin's "idiosyncratic Russian"[7] (Raskin 1981: 667), and, in her preface to *Problems of Dostoevsky's Poetics*, Caryl Emerson describes his style as a kind of transcribed speech. In her words,

> one is in fact surprised to discover how comfortably Bakhtin can be read aloud. He has that generous inefficiency characteristic of certain oral genres. Like an epic singer, he presents his concepts in formulaic groupings of words; by italicizing key phrases he seems to emphasize an almost spoken accent. His prose is sprinkled with conversational markers, and he is at

times capricious with punctuation. Sentences of enormous and undifferentiated length pile up (Bakhtin 1984a:xxxiii).

Bakhtin employed a number of unusual expressions ("heteroglossia," "dialogism," "chronotope," "monoglossia," and so forth) and used them at times with little or no explanation. His heavy neologisms and often technical vocabulary present interpreters with a number of obstacles, but it is important to take his words seriously.[8] And finally, Bakhtin's formulations are original, but often unsystematic. He covers a vast range of topics in an eclectic manner, and his scattered style of writing underscores his way of thinking.

BAKHTIN'S PLACE IN LITERARY HISTORY

In an attempt to gain a philosophical and methodological framework for Bakhtin's contribution, one might begin by asking how his ideas contrast with various literary schools of thought. David Penchansky (1990:10-19) and Terry Eagleton (1983:91-150) conveniently summarize Formalism, Marxism, and Deconstructionism in their books. Where does Bakhtin fit in? He lived from 1895 to 1975, and anyone familiar with literary history would assume that he could be conveniently placed in the camp of the Russian Formalists. Though their contemporary, Bakhtin was not one of them. His own ideas are less polemical than theirs, and he suggests that they made a mistake by treating texts as mere objects to be studied, or as repositories for formal, linguistic analysis: "In a word, formalism is not able to admit that an external social factor acting on literature could become an intrinsic factor of literature itself, a factor of immanent development" (Medvedev/Bakhtin 1978:67). Bakhtin offers an informed and energetic response to the more rigid tendencies of Russian Formalist thought. His ultimate goal is to elucidate the constantly emerging form of the novel, and this objective is accomplished by moving into the realm of folkloristics. In much less technocratic fashion, Bakhtin views texts in *personal* terms, as places where communication is possible. A relationship is formed when characters address an audience; that is, when an *I* addresses a *You*. While the Formalists were autonomizing and sealing off literary texts from their broader socio-historical context, Bakhtin was working to open them up.

By linking concrete utterances to particular social contexts, Bakhtin displays some similarity in thought with the Marxists of his day who stressed social and historical specificity. He admits that there is no language which is not part of definite social relations, and that this matrix is in turn part of broader political and economic systems. Bakhtin did describe Rabelais as a "deeply revolutionary spirit," but the observation is made not as an attack against the bourgeoisie per se. Instead, Rabelais reacts to any kind of intellectual stasis, moral fixity, or neatly ordered system. Revolution, for Bakhtin, is "a dramatic thrust for perpetual renewal, for confounding canons, for randomness and diversity" (Clark and Holquist 1984:316). By highlighting what he calls the "dialogic"—the word is related both to dialogue and dialectic nature of language, Bakhtin suggests that utterances are active components of speech more than fixed units or fixed signs. Utterances are masks—masks that cannot claim to be completely unambiguous representations of the self or some other "objective" reality—which are affected by specific social conditions. In short, language is not a monolithic system but a source of ideological potential with multiple possibilities in heterogeneous societies. But Bakhtin rejects the view espoused by some Marxists that literature is a mere report on society or a barometer of movement and change due to conflict. For Bakhtin, such a reductionist aspect of Marxist thought is shortsighted because literature in its linguistic makeup reflects social idioms, not social facts. These idioms bear testimony to different ideologies, and artistic discourse is not a simple, direct reflection of economic life.

Some of Bakhtin's philosophical remarks might just as well have been made by the Deconstructionists. His views on "dialogized" discourse exhibit some surprising similarities to the work of Jacques Derrida, Michel Foucault, and Jacques Lacan, who suggest that language displays a "surplus" over exact meaning. The common thread between Bakhtin and their thought is the shared concept of language as "dialogized," that is, always changing and never hermetically sealed. A text for Bakhtin is a locus of verbal interchange, and he denies text, reader, or author a place of priority. Yet Bakhtin is no Deconstructionist either, as his emphasis on authors makes clear. A central idea found in many of his writings is that two types of novels exist: the "mono-logic," where an author speaks for the characters, and the "dia-logic," where the voice of the author is not superior to any character's voice (cf. Gunn and Fewell 1993:6-7, 165-73).

Bakhtin, therefore, cannot be too closely identified with any single school of thought, and attempts to place him, as helpful (and common) as the pigeonholing practice is, are in this case unfair, if not futile. This thinker moves back and forth between the boundaries of Russian Formalism and contemporary critical theory. Paul de Man described Bakhtin's appeal to theoreticians in diverse fields at a recent Modern Language Association meeting. Bakhtin appeals to so many diverse groups, de Man wryly observed, that virtually no one would have trouble enlisting his insight "to defend just about anything" (Carroll 1983: 67). To Bakhtin's credit, many issues in philosophy of language and linguistics that are discussed today were evident in the 1929 edition of his work on Dostoevsky.

TEXTS AS SOCIAL PHENOMENA

At the foundation of Bakhtin's enterprise is the idea that literary works are social phenomena. In his essay, "Discourse in the Novel," Bakhtin writes,

> the study of verbal art can and must overcome the divorce be-
> tween an abstract "formal" approach and an equally abstract
> "ideological" approach. Form and content in discourse are
> one, once we understand that verbal discourse is a social
> phenomenon—social throughout its entire range and in each
> and every of its factors, from the sound image to the furthest
> reaches of abstract meaning (1981:259).

Bakhtin understands artistic discourse as an inalienable part, but a transformable part, of a larger whole, and his concept of language as the product of an open and at times conflicting social interaction (rather than a product of universal laws) overcomes the weakness of Formalism and Structuralism.

Texts, biblical or otherwise, are part of the total body of social discourse carried out from day to day and from era to era. Such views form the basis for what he calls "sociological stylistics." In Bakhtin's words,

> the internal social dialogism of . . . discourse requires the concrete social context of discourse to be exposed, to be revealed as the force that determines its entire stylistic structure, its "form" and its "content," determining it not from without, but from within; for indeed, social dialogue reverberates in all aspects of discourse, in those relating to "content" as well as the "formal" aspects themselves (1981:300).

Language is made up of words which acquire accents, tones, meanings, voices, intentions, and idioms. These words have their own histories, their own previous and future significations. The interaction and fluid nature of language is what Bakhtin means by "the dialogical." Words on the page or words in the air are hybrid in nature: they acquire meaning in a localized setting of speakers and writers as well as in social and historical environments where utterances exist. Such dialogue is an inherent quality of language. Thus, words are something other than lexical elements. They gain in meaning only as they are contextualized and situated, and because words reflect non-homogenous social ideological forces, readers will not always agree on a text's ideological point of view. If we are socially minded enough to use Bakhtin's method, interpretation of literary texts becomes somewhat personal. Joel Rosenberg says it well when he writes that "most of us are so used to the idea that interpretation is something we do *to* literature, that we forget the *extent* to which it is the other way around: that literature interprets *us*" (1975:67; original emphasis).

Form and content, sign and history, text and interpretation—they are all viewed as parts of a thoroughly social process of verbal intercourse. "We are taking language," Bakhtin observes, "not as a system of abstract grammatical categories, but rather language conceived as ideologically saturated, language as a worldview, even as a concrete opinion, ensuring a *maximum* of mutual understanding in all spheres of ideological life"

(1981:271; original emphasis). Such language that is "ideologically saturated" sends ideas running back and forth between partners in dialogue who work for maximum understanding. With language understood as a social construct, meaning cannot be formalized because dialogue, as Bakhtin understands it, can never be fully specified. Bakhtin's name for this kind of boundlessness is "heteroglossia." As social and historical conditions are taken into account in interpretive acts, words spoken or written at any given time and place reflect different meanings, to either a small or large degree, from what they might if spoken at other historical moments and in other contexts. Because of this "heteroglossic" element of human utterances, interpreters influenced by conditions other than those at the time of the original speech event may never fully recover the primal or core meaning of previous semantic moments. Interpreters can never take into full account the decisive interplay between "centripetal" and "centrifugal" agencies in a particular language and culture, on the one hand, and innovative or "idiolectic" uses of language by individuals on the other (1981:272-273). To speak, to write, and to read, Bakhtin teaches, is to apprehend the relative, open-ended nature of semantic phenomena.

While Bakhtin is suggesting that texts and interpretations are social constructs, he is not advancing the view that meaning is indeterminate—as his analysis of Dickens' *Little Dorrit* (1981: 302-309) or of Tolstoy's "Three Deaths" (1984a:69-73), for example, makes clear. Meaning is, instead, ever-burgeoning. Every speech or sign is dialogically ever-available for re-interpretation from an always more complex point of view. The past can never be considered closed or hegemonized in meaning because the past and present continue to affect each other in new and often unpredictable ways. To varying extents, then, all interpreters re-form, con-form, and de-form the stories they read and hear according to their perspectives, their objectives, and their life experiences.

BAKHTIN AND THE NOVEL

Bakhtin attributed enormous significance to art, particularly to the novel, as a means for expressing ideas inaccessible to rational or philosophical discourse. He discusses the nature and evolution of the novel in four essays that he wrote in the 1930s and 1940s. The titles of these essays are: "Epic and the Novel," "From the Prehistory of Novelistic Discourse," "Forms of Time and of the Chronotope in the Novel," and "Discourse in the Novel."[9] Bakhtin's thesis about the novel is simple, even if his style is not. The novel, assimilating so many characteristics of other genres, eventually emerges as the gauge of social voices of different eras. It is the supreme literary genre because in it all previous major genres, the epic in particular, find their natural fulfillment. In addition, it is the supreme art form for Bakhtin because it dramatizes the spirit of parody, highlights social heteroglossia, and most importantly, represents life as open-ended, incomplete, and beyond formal or systematic description. With the novel genre, the protagonist engages in a process of discovery as a human being, a subjectivity full of personal experiences and ideological initiative. It is precisely because the novel is an open-ended genre reflecting shifts in perception in a more comprehensive fashion than other art forms that it provides Bakhtin ample opportunity to formulate ideas about language and social theory (Clark and Holquist 1984:294).

Bakhtin defines literary evolution in terms of two categories. Static or closed genres, such as the epic, are viewed as confined to an "absolute past" (Bakhtin 1984a:108), complete in themselves and out of sync with contemporary time. Open genres, on the other hand, such as the novel in its multiple forms (from Greek times to the present), are capable of organic development. The open genre reaches its high point in what he calls the polyphonic, or "multi-voiced," novel, first written, according to Bakhtin at least, by Dostoevsky. Dostoevsky's single greatest accomplishment is the multiple autonomous centers he created in his narrative worlds. In contrast to Dostoevsky's works, the "monologic" novel features one voice, that of the author as the evaluative and dominating voice over all others in the work. The monologic novelist—Leo Tolstoy is the writer Bakhtin mentions on multiple occasions—strives to create a "compact and unambiguous whole" (Bakhtin 1984a:203). On the other hand, in Dostoevsky's work, one encounters a polyphony of independent voices that are not overcome by a dominating monologic position of the author.

But what impact does Bakhtin's view of the novel have on the ancient story known as Esther? Bakhtin brings to his discussion thoughts that bear on the entire history of verbal discourse, and he clearly does not mean by novel a particular type of writing that begins with Cervantes, DeFoe, or Fielding. Dostoevsky's momentous achievement is prepared for by centuries of development: "The . . . novel of the nineteenth century is only one of the branches—and a rather impoverished and deformed branch at that—of a powerful and multi-branched generic tradition, reaching, as we have said, into the depths of the past, to the very sources of European literature" (Bakhtin 1984a: 105-106). Bakhtin almost names Socrates as the first novelist because of the emphasis on self-consciousness and the role of dialogue in his philosophical discourses. That Bakhtin is interested in the novel as it developed over centuries and not just in the novel as an art form may also be seen in his appeal to the menippean satire (see "The Serio-comical" section in chapter 2). After cataloguing a number of generic features of menippean satire, Bakhtin concludes that while these writers did not yet know "polyphony," the distinguishing characteristics of their writings—the fantastic and adventure, combined comic elements, philosophical reflection, *skandal* scenes characterized by eccentric behavior—paved the way for the full-blown polyphonic novel. Socratic dialogues and the menippean satires were both conducive to Dostoevsky's novel, though Bakhtin is quick to point out that Dostoevsky did not proceed "directly" or "consciously" from the ancient genres (1984a:121). Bakhtin, then, is actually concerned with something other than *the novel*. According to Clark and Holquist, the novel is not just a literary genre for Bakhtin, "but a special kind of force, which he calls 'novelness'" (1984:276). Bakhtin believes that other genres may be novelized or novelistic and that certain long works of prose fiction are actually not novelistic at all. He is able to discover novelistic discourse in socratic dialogue and menippean satire because they present the image of multiple voices and interanimating languages.

At the heart of the novelistic is quoted speech. In fact, Bakhtin defines the genre as "a diversity of individual voices, artistically organized" (1981:262). The novel is structured in terms of dialogue, and while other genres disguise or repress this trait to varying extents, the novel's open-ended capacity to consolidate different kinds and levels of speech sets it apart from the relatively closed or "monologic" voices of poetry.

In his essay, "From the Prehistory of Novelistic Discourse," Bakhtin examines ancient and medieval literary genres—including biblical parodies, Greek romances and parodies, and grammatical treatises—in an attempt to chart the development of the emerging novel. The mixing of languages, what Bakhtin calls polyglossia, and the importance of laughter are prominent subjects in his discussion. Unique utterance combinations and forms of carnival are social phenomena that literature reflects. When Bakhtin turns to Rabelais, he relates thoughts on these and other formal characteristics directly to festivity, including ancient feasts and medieval holiday carnivals. He also identifies similar themes of festivity in literature such as the glorification of the body or the celebration of intoxication.

ESTHER, BAKHTIN, AND THE NOVEL

Justification for associating Bakhtin to a tradition as old as the Esther story may emerge more clearly when we read this passage from *The Dialogic Imagination*:

> We speak of a special novelistic discourse because it is only in the novel that discourse can reveal all its specific potential and achieve its true depth. But the novel is a comparatively recent genre. Indirect discourse, however, the representation of another's word, another's language in intonational quotation marks, was known in the most ancient times; we encounter it in the earliest stages of verbal culture. . . . These diverse forms prepared the ground for the novel long before its actual appearance. Novelistic discourse has a lengthy prehistory, going back centuries, even thousands of years (1981:50).

With the novel understood in this broad sense and with its inception set at a very early period, we may ask how the story of Esther relates to this framework. Of course, one can think of many reasons for separating an author such as Rabelais or Dostoevsky from the author of the Esther story: differences in language, time, culture, and so forth. On what grounds may insight be drawn from Bakhtin? He does refer to the New Testament (1981: 69-70, 179; 1984a:15, 16, 135, 142, 155-56, 275, 280), but mentions the Hebrew Bible only in passing (1984a:15, 280; 1984b: 227). The first reason is, perhaps, that we cannot resurrect the ancient writers to ask them how *they* understood their trade. No writing survives from ancient Israel quite like Aristotle's systematic study of literature in the *Poetics*. But more justification can be found. While Bakhtin is most widely known as a theorist of the novel, his understanding of "the novelistic," dialogue, and *skandal* scenes has direct implications for the Esther scroll.

My concern is not so much to praise Bakhtin as to make worthwhile use of certain aspects of his work that seem particularly illuminating for the ancient story. A number of commentators have explored the story's great "literary art;"[10] some have even described it as a "novel," (Loader 1978:417-21), a "novella" (White 1992:125; Hallo 1983:25), or a "novelle" (Siegel 1985:142-51). My purpose is to ask *in what way* is the story of Esther linked to the novel—the novel, that is, as Bakhtin understands it—and to ask if the biblical story is an example of the literary carnivalesque.

THE ESTHER TALES

In this study I propose to isolate a few major ideas that are found in Bakhtin's writings and to ask if they shed any light on the story(-ies) of Esther. The discussion will focus on the interpretive richness of language as informed by Bakhtin, but, due to the size of his work and even more to the kind of discourse that he has generated in aesthetics, philosophy of language, and social theory, there is much that this study cannot provide. I will draw from the primary sources of Bakhtin's writings, especially from *Rabelais and His World*, and from the Hebrew version of the Esther story. My major objective is to show that it is an early example of the literary carnivalesque. Before moving on to an analysis of these narratives, a few final words about interpretation may be helpful.

The notion that all readings are shaped by culture, values, worldviews—or in a word, ideology—is certainly not confined to Bakhtin. In fact, a number of scholars working in the area of biblical studies have recently stressed this idea to show, among other things, that patriarchy as a social construct has influenced interpretation of biblical texts, often resulting in the subjugation of women in the name of religious orthodoxy (Ruether 1983). A convincing case has also been put forth that certain problems of androcentric narratives stem not only from the text themselves, but also from the literary imagination that one brings to the text, an imagination that is often informed by androcentric or patriarchal paradigms (Fiorenza 1984).[11]

With respect to the biblical story of Esther, one indication of culture's shifting role in interpretation is suggested by radically different views of the roles of Vashti and Esther in the narrative. For example, in the Hebrew version of the story, the action opens like this: King Ahasuerus throws a party for his officials and ministers. Nobles, governors, and members of the Persian[12] army are present. During the one hundred and eighty day party, the king displays his great wealth (1:4). When the festivities end, Ahasuerus gives a seven day banquet for all the people of Susa. When the king becomes "merry with wine" (v. 10), he resolves once again to show off. This time he decides to display his wife, Queen Vashti, to the people. She, however, refuses to comply with the king's command. One of Ahasuerus's advisers, Memucan, concludes that Vashti's response will likely influence "all" the women throughout the kingdom. He advises the king to take quick and decisive action against Vashti so that "all women will give honor to their husbands" (v. 20). So King Ahasuerus puts aside Vashti for insubordination. He then orders a beauty contest. The virgins of the empire are called into his court, and then into his bedchamber. Esther wins the favor of the king, becomes the new queen, and, in the chapters that follow, plays a crucial part in the unfolding plot. After learning of Haman's plan to slaughter all the Jews in the Persian empire, Esther appears unsummoned before the king. She foils Haman's plot. Haman is executed.

Interpreters have understood Esther's and Vashti's roles in

this story in different ways. S. Paul Re'emi concludes, in a rather matter-of-fact tone, that Vashti refused the king "possibly because she found it indecent or forbidden by a Persian law of modesty" (Coggins and Re'emi 1985:117). But neither the text nor Re'emi cites such a "law of modesty." Dorothea Harvey, author of the *Interpreter's Dictionary of the Bible* article on Vashti, suggests that the queen's role in the book may be "simply a fictional device for introducing Esther" (1962:747). Neither Harvey nor Re'emi—not to mention a host of others— alludes to the distinct possibility which the text allows: Vashti refuses because she does not wish to be displayed on stage at her drunken husband's request. Or consider the way that Esther has also been viewed in different ways. It is Mordecai who is sometimes described as "the major character" of the story. G. Mercati, for example, asks why the book was named after Esther when Mordecai is the principal character (Bickerman 1967:171, 235 n. 1), and Carey Moore states that "between Mordecai and Esther the greater hero in the Hebrew is Mordecai, who supplied the brains while Esther simply followed his directions" (Moore 1971:lii). What?! It is Esther who becomes queen in this Persian court, who outmaneuvers Haman, the king's vizier who had endangered her life. It is Esther who not only saves her life by bringing Haman to the gallows, but also the lives of her own people. Esther gains power despite the fact that she, a woman, would have found herself virtually powerless in patriarchal Persia. It is Esther who succeeds by dealing with and overcoming those who hold power in this story. She combines courage and ingenuity and wins her way by her own initiatives. Like so many women who appear in the stories of the Bible, she works around and through the powers that be in order to save herself, and in this case her people also. If Mordecai is the major character, why did someone name the story for Esther (cf. Gunn and Fewell 1993:76, 79-81)?

This is not to say, however, that interpreters have consistently downplayed Esther or Vashti's actions, or that all have exalted Mordecai as the true hero of the tale. According to Jack Sasson, it is Esther who has the "most personal voice of any character" in the story. She shows her genuine concern for her

cousin in 4:4 and reveals the burden that she carries on behalf
of the people in 4:16. At the second banquet, she "flatters,
pleads, deplores, then turns sarcastic . . . all within two verses"
(Sasson 1987:337). In similar fashion, Johanna Bos (1986:43)
asserts that the only character who is developed through the
story is that of Esther. Frieda Hyman calls Esther the "one ster-
ling character" of the story (1986:85), and Sidnie Ann White
describes Vashti as a "strong female character who loses her position as a result of her refusal to acquiesce to the greater society's demands upon her" (1992:127). These radically different
views on the role of Vashti and Esther are enough to suggest
that interpretation is a culturally influenced social phenomenon.

Another important issue related to interpretation is transmis-
sion of the story. Like so many books of the Bible, the textual
history of Esther is quite complex. Part of this complexity can be
explained by the fact that the story survives in a Hebrew tradition as well as in two distinct Greek text traditions.[13] Virtually
all researchers, Clines excepted (1984), have focused on one or
occasionally two of the Esther stories.[14] The three versions of
the Esther story may be designated as the M, B, and A texts.
The M (or MT) story has received the most attention from the
scholarly community, but a number of historical questions, such
as the date of (final) composition—Moore (1971:lix) suggests a
wide range of dates, 400-114 B.C.E.—has not been settled. The
B-text (or LXX version) includes six passages (usually called
"additions") that are not found in the Hebrew text. These
passages, designated A-F in many Bibles, are interspersed
through the Greek translation and gathered as a separate book
in the Apocrypha ("The Additions to the Book of Esther").
When compared to the M story, the chain of events in the
B-text presents a different portrait of Esther and the other
characters. According to Clines, these six passages increase the
M version "by more than two-thirds" (1984:70). These so-called
additions were written at different times and in different places.
Most of them were *probably*—this is as precise as we can
be—written sometime during the second century B.C.E. (Moore
1977:13). Sections B, E, and possibly F were originally com-
posed in Greek, while sections C and D were most likely first

written in Hebrew or Aramaic. The origin of the A section is uncertain (Fox 1991:265-266). The Esther story survives in yet a third tradition, the so-called A-text which is preserved in five Greek manuscripts (MSS 19, 93, 108, 319, and 392). David Clines's treatment (1984) is the most comprehensive to date on these three Esther stories, and he provides the first complete translation of the A-text into any language. At times, passages from the A-text mirror the narration and speech found in the B-text. At other times, however, particularly at the end, A is quite unlike B.

The story of Esther then exists in multiple literary traditions. Except for occasional adjustments based on the original languages, the NRSV translation is followed in this study. Since language is decisive, even the choice of texts to read and to quote has implications in a study on ideology because the process of translating from one language to another requires that interpretive decisions be made. A shift in culture's understanding of language is, for example, nowhere more apparent than in the NRSV, which avoids exclusive, time-honored masculine words and images that have been used to refer to people.[15] Thus several factors suggest that many more than three Esther stories (M, B, and A) exist: the burgeoning translations of these texts into many languages, modifications to translations within a single language family (the RSV and the NRSV, for example), shifts in cultural readings, and so forth.

The Esther stories are narratives conveyed by several voices, and through the representation of events we gain a multi-faceted perspective of the action. The authors are artists who manage the telling, and, in turn, shape audiences' responses. The characters are revealed, not only in terms of the evaluative system of authors, but also from the point of view of other characters' actions and words. Yet the Esther stories are also social phenomena because they generate new discourses in new contexts for every new reader. A few questions arise from this brief survey: Why does this story of Esther survive as the stories of Esther? Why does an ancient (or modern) author (or culture) decide to perform radical surgery on a text? Or why is a story supplemented with narrative blocks subsequently? A major difference, and perhaps the major difference, between the Hebrew tale of Esther and the Greek stories is that the Hebrew lacks "religious" language and themes. (We shall return to this point.) In general terms, two ancient stories of Esther survived: one with a decidedly "secular" appearance (i.e., the Hebrew version), and another which is decidedly religious in tone, language, and theme (i.e., the Greek). Again, a few questions come to mind: *Why* does a gulf exist separating the two? On what grounds have interpreters dismissed or even argued for removing the "secular" Hebrew story from the canon?

Herein lies the real task of this study: to discover how individual words, phrases, and speech units carry ideology in the Hebrew story. Such a full-working view will illustrate that the Esther tale is an aesthetic as well as a social text where content is produced within an ideological frame. Multiple ideological viewpoints suggest a fairly complex network of relationships, and content itself emerges as a player in the ideological game. The technical choices that the author of the Esther (M) story makes throughout betray values and judgments that are available to anyone who reads or hears the story, and the psychological and ideological relationships among narrator, characters, narrative events, author, and audience give rise to a full-blown ideological system. The story has multiplied, and, if Bakhtin is right, even the canonical texts are not really frozen. Language does not congeal to produce an immobile system, and, even if the traditions were frozen, the texts await further re-interpretation—as the conflicting views of Vashti and Esther's roles in the story make clear—because Esther's audience is always in flux.

This discussion then leads to the heart of the issue: in bypassing the Hebrew Bible and declaring throughout *Rabelais and His World*, *Problems of Dostoevsky's Poetics*, and the four essays included in *The Dialogic Imagination* that authors long before the post-Renaissance novel dealt with the dynamic, self-subverting, always open-ended flux of life, Bakhtin left a door wide open. Heteroglossia, dialogic spontaneity, and the carnivalesque may all be a part of the biblical tradition. Esther provides us a test case, as we explore the literary carnivalesque.

2

THE
LITERARY
CARNIVALESQUE

B akhtin, the theoretician, is also quite concerned with folk culture, epitomized in his view by carnival. Carnival celebrations predate Christianity, and have their roots in pre-class society as a celebration of life in the community. Carnival extends a kind of general hegemony over people, places, even time. "While carnival lasts," Bakhtin writes, "there is no other life outside it. During carnival time life is subject only to . . . the laws of its own freedom" (1984b:7). According to Bakhtin's scenario, carnivals develop in response to "official," oppressive forces. The carnival occasion is provocative because it imitates an alternative view of reality and embodies a liberating escape from the status quo. Bakhtin holds a utopian view of carnival that suspends "all hierarchical rank, privileges, norms, and prohibitions" (1984b:10), and the horizontal and egalitarian structures of carnival lower the hierarchy of an official culture or an official force. Since dominant ideologies seek to establish a unified and fixed social order, carnival is always a threat. Carnivals are celebrated as a feast for all the world in the public square,[1] and the key image is "pregnant death," a designation that highlights the ambivalent nature of life itself: destruction and uncrowning are related to birth and renewal; death is linked to regeneration; all the images of carnival are connected to the paradox of the dying and the reborn world. Symbols of change and renewal highlight the rejection of prevailing truths and authorities.

During a period of centuries, this unique social phenomenon becomes a literary phenomenon as well. In a far reaching claim, Bakhtin unites carnival and the novel, and argues that both the carnival and the novel worlds are parodic and ambivalent. The attitude prevalent in carnival ritual, with its communal task of seeing the world, is fundamental to the development of the novel. The special carnival form of symbol and metaphor evolved as a rich idiom reflecting the varied experiences of the people, and the open-ended nature of carnival forms to the dynamics of social change enabled their further historical development in literature. Certain experiences, opposed to all that was ready-made, found dynamic expressions. Authors developed new, ever-changing, and playful forms. In Bakhtin's words, "these [carnivalesque] forms developed during thousands of years [and] served the new historic aims of the epoch; they were filled with powerful historic awareness and led to a deeper understanding of reality" (1984b:208).

Bakhtin calls this development "the carnivalization of literature" (1984a:122), and its analysis makes up the principal content of his book *Rabelais and His World*. In his study of carnival's influence on literature, Bakhtin emphasizes a complex interplay between the "official" world and the world of carnival release. "Ambivalence" and "joyful relativity" are favorite terms. Carnival or festive license does not simply consist of an inversion of everyday norms, a strict opposition to official culture. It expresses instead "the inevitability and at the same time the creative power of the shift-and-renewal, the *joyful relativity* of all structure and order" (1984a:124; original emphasis). Carnivalization is not an external form imposed upon or adapted to ideas; the transformation is rather what Bakhtin calls "an extraordinarily flexible form of artistic visualization, a peculiar sort of heuristic principle making possible the discovery of new and as yet unseen things" (1984a:166). By relativizing all that is externally stable, carnivalization, with its unique emphasis, allows writers and readers to explore the deepest layers of human relationships.

This literature has its own idiom and is especially rich in a marketplace style of expression. Rituals are associated with the carnivalesque (both in its social and literary expressions), such as the pairing of opposites or reversals: crownings and un-crownings, male – female, king – fool, womb – tomb, and de-basements – exaltations. A unitary and complex carnival percep-tion of the world permeates carnival stories, and this literature has its own logic, the peculiar logic of parody and travesty, of the "inside out" and the "turnabout" with continual shifts from top to bottom, and from front to rear. It is impossible to trans-late this concrete-sensual language completely and adequately into a verbal language or into a language of abstract concepts.

Bakhtin sees the late Renaissance as the final great manifes-tation of carnival in Europe, but, like the novel, it is preceded by centuries of development. He does not discuss the Hebrew Bible in this context, but, as the dissolution of hierarchies and authorities as well as the reversals mentioned above suggest, his understanding of the carnivalesque has a number of implica-tions for our study. The plot of Esther often reveals an inverted logic, and the story is characterized by a number of reversals. Haman ends up on the gallows that he had built for Mordecai. Female Esther emerges as the hero of the story in this male dominated narrative world. Mordecai outthinks the not-so-reflective King Ahasuerus. Established hierarchies, reigning au-thorities, and worldviews are all destroyed in Esther's narrative world. We may, indeed, be in the world of carnivalesque folk-lore.

Bakhtin comes to the conclusion that carnival developed an entire language of symbolic forms—from large and complex group performances to individual carnival gestures. These forms not only provide the historical key to an author's signs and images; they also provide a key to meaning. The major image and defining form of carnival is the festival itself. The plot, images, and tone are all shaped by a free-jolly festival atmo-sphere. The festival, the beliefs associated with it, and its unique atmosphere of freedom and merriment transpose everyday life to make the impossible possible. The Esther (M) narrative soon became (and may have been designed as) a festal reading, and a number of important scenes are directly related to feasting and festivity. The Hebrew version of the story begins (1:1-9) and ends (9:16-19) with a feast, and crucial turning points in the plot are marked by drinking: the selection of Queen Esther (2:18), the edict to destroy the Jews (3:15), Esther's plan to unmask Haman (5:4-14; 7:1-10), and the rejoicing at the favorable decree (8:17). This action is imbued with a carnivalesque atmosphere where virtually all the episodes are presented by the author in the popular-festive carnival spirit.

The spirit of carnival derives from folk culture and folk humor, and this unique combination of culture and humor thrives in the open tent and the marketplace. Bakhtin's interest lies in a fundamental struggle between folk culture and an official, dominating culture of the Renaissance, and he lays heaviest stress on an author's freedom to play with authorized symbols and solemn institutions of the day. The high language of the "poet, scholar, monk, knight" is parodied in irreverent play in the marketplace and square. The folk exploit and overturn hierarchy and the "single language of truth" (Clark and Holquist 1984:272). The Renaissance, with all its Michelangelos and Queen Elizabeths, is mainly distinguished by the manner in which its greatest figures—Shakespeare, Cervantes, Rabelais—satirize official culture by drawing upon carnivalesque sources of folk humor. The folk express the attitudes and aspirations of a non-oppressive future and give literature its progressive, utopian cast in the Renaissance. In his understanding of the future, life, death, and power, Bakhtin suggests that the folk assume the role of superhumans who transcend history. In times of regimentation, carnival—whether ancient, medieval, or modern—celebrates freedom. In times of authoritarianism and dogmatism, the folk respond with ebullient and irreverent play. In the story of Esther, it is Haman, eager to destroy an entire race because Mordecai will not bow down to him, who is outwitted by the powerless heroes of the folk, Esther and Mordecai.[2]

In response to dogmatism or temporary revolutions, folk laughter organizes carnival in a transhistorical manner. This laughter rises above the objects at which it is aimed. It seeks to decrown, it seeks to transform all that is official and sacred. It is the common folk of town and country who delight in improprieties. *They* are the ones who turn existing structures upside down. "We cannot understand cultural and literary life and the struggle of [hu]mankind's historic past," Bakhtin writes in his book on Rabelais (1984b:474), "if we ignore that peculiar folk humor that always existed and was never merged with the official culture of the ruling classes." Folk logic has its own philosophical, aesthetic, and ideological essence. The folk provide a healthy antidote to those who are stodgy, pompous, official, or monologic. Amid the hurly-burly of political life, Bakhtin asserts, only the folk are able to view life in all its joyful relativity. By ridiculing death and finiteness, folk culture refuses to acknowledge official institutions and authority by denying official power and its hierarchical rigor. Through the enactment of unique carnival gestures and rituals, the folk staged this drama. In the chapters that follow, I seek to examine what I believe is a folk-carnivalistic base that has been collected and artistically rendered as the Hebrew Esther narrative. Indeed, this social and literary document is an early example of "the carnivalization of literature."

RABELAIS AND HISTORICAL POETICS

Bakhtin places Renaissance culture in a special place in the history of writing. His main theme is that folk culture and high culture merge at this time. In the Renaissance the boundary between official and unofficial worlds is suspended, and laughing voices are heard in the lowest and highest spheres of literature: "In the Renaissance, laughter in its most radical, universal, and at the same time gay form emerged from the depths of folk culture; it emerged but once in the course of history, over a period of some fifty or sixty years (in various countries and at various times) and entered with its popular (vulgar) language the sphere of great literature and high ideology" (1984b:72). In addition, ancient authors (such as Lucian, Plutarch, and Macrobius) are also representatives of this tendency toward carnival. Indeed, for Bakhtin the relationship between this antique carnival and the Renaissance is a close one.

> Rabelais and his contemporaries were also familiar, of course, with the antique conception of laughter from other sources—from Athenaeus, Macrobius, and others. They knew Homer's famous words about the undestroyable, that is, eternal laugh-

ter of the gods, and they were familiar with the Roman tradition of the freedom of laughter during the Saturnalia and the role of laughter during the triumphal marches and the funeral rites of notables. Rabelais in particular makes frequent allusion to these sources. . . . A millennium of folk humor broke into Renaissance literature. This thousand-year-old laughter not only fertilized literature but was itself fertilized by humanist knowledge and advanced literary techniques (1984b: 70, 72).

Bakhtin sees in the Renaissance not only the fusion of antique carnival and the folk culture of the Middle Ages, but also the historically unique phenomenon of folk culture overcoming high culture.

In *Rabelais and His World*, Bakhtin makes a good deal of the folk. "In all world literature," Bakhtin writes, "there is probably no other work reflecting so fully and deeply all aspects of the life of the marketplace as does Rabelais's novel [*Gargantua and Pantagruel*]" (1984b: 154). Rabelais writes a hymn for the common man and woman (i.e., for the folk, those non-stodgy, non-official members of society), and reconstructs this folk culture in its verbal and ritual manifestations through an analysis of *Gargantua and Pantagruel*. Rabelais's work is, of course, infamous for its massive breaches of decorum, its scatological detail, bizarre allusions, and intermingling of high brow vocabularies with the crudest billingsgate. Bakhtin's basic contention is that Rabelais reassembles the pieces of the medieval world and provides a new foundation, one which is based not on real time and space, as much as on non-eschatological motifs that celebrate the physical side of life on a cosmic scale. Rabelais is not concealing seriousness in scatological tales; his roguish peasant-kings are authentic folk heroes, and Rabelais is their literary voice and ideological advocate. Rabelais's work exposes the cultural and semantic context of the Renaissance, a unique period where folk culture and high culture converge. Three political villains—the bourgeoisie, the Holy Roman Empire, and the major villain, the Roman Catholic Church—threatened the cultural climate at the time of Rabelais. It is Rabelais who fights them off using only the weapon of folk humor.

Bakhtin contends that the experiences of folk culture derive from a conflict with official culture. The concrete expressions invented by folk culture oppose the official forms of the time, and with Rabelais we witness the incursion of folk humor, with its irreverent, ambivalent, and universal play. This boisterous, festive hilarity of Renaissance carnival is invested with a kind of laughter that has philosophical meaning, a "universal and philosophic character" that testifies to a "gay relativity of prevailing truths and authorities" (1984b:133, 99), and Rabelais uses festive modes to shatter, rather than to rebuild, preexisting literary molds.

All acts of world history are accompanied by a laughing chorus. Though Rabelais led the laughing chorus of popular culture during only one period of time, the Renaissance, he revealed the language of laughing people with such clarity and fullness of voice that his work sheds light on folk culture and humor of other ages. (Laughter, especially the form derived from folk culture, is also, I shall argue in chapter 6, an integral part of the Hebrew Esther story.) Basing his argument on historical data, Bakhtin locates the apex of carnival in Renaissance life and literature: "Beginning with the seventeenth century, folk-carnival life is on the wane: it almost loses touch with communal performance, its specific weight in the life of people is sharply reduced, its forms are impoverished, made petty and less complex" (1984a:130). In the late Renaissance and thereafter, when folk carnivals lose their force, "carnival almost completely ceases to be a direct source of carnivalization, ceding its place to the influence of already carnivalized literature; in this way carnivalization becomes a purely literary tradition" (1984a: 131).

Bakhtin concludes that all of the carnivalesque elements of Rabelais's novels—the menippea, Socratic dialogue, the diatribe, the soliloquy, and the confession—reached Rabelais only after a long developmental process. The essential folk-carnivalistic base expanded and was enriched, but, despite some modifications, these elements retained their primary nucleus. By the time of Rabelais, carnival acquired new meaning when it absorbed the hopes and thoughts of the people from one generation to the next. Even as carnival language and images developed, the generic core remained intact and discernible.

While the carnivalesque has its roots in ancient culture, it only emerges in those moments in history when decentralization of a culture has undermined the authority of social establishments, national myths, and correct languages. Several questions arise: Did the carnival impulse arise at all for the ancient author of the Hebrew Esther narrative? Did this ancient author desire to subvert and demonstrate the falsity of socially instituted ideologies? Do we find in Esther many of the elements, even in a subdued form, of carnival life: the clownish crownings and uncrownings, the lavish banquets, the contrast between official and non-official culture, the persistent fool, rogue, and simpleton, the theme of death and dying, and so forth? Such carnivalistic images are, indeed, found in Esther as well as in Rabelais's world. The carnivalesque crowd from ancient Persia or from the Renaissance, in the marketplace or in the street, is not merely a crowd. It is a group of people organized in their own way, the way of the folk. Bakhtin's description of carnival's system of language serves as a lens through which to view Esther's narrative world. If Renaissance carnival was the high point of at least a millennia-long development, Esther may be part, a very early part, of this historical process.

THE SERIO-COMICAL GENRE

Bakhtin divides literature into two stylistic categories. The first is the serious type, heroic and full of pathos. Examples include the epic, tragedy, history, and rhetoric. The second type is what he calls the serio-comical, a term derived from the ancient Greeks who identified the *spoudogeloios* ("serious-smiling") genre. Examples include the mimes of Sophron, the Socratic dialogue, the literature of the Symposiasts, the memoir literature of Critias and Ion of Chios, and "Menippean Satires."[3] Neither type of writing can reduce experience to a monolithic tragic or comic vision. Serio-comical authors can, however, distance themselves from the language of their work through humorous, ironic, and satiric accents as they undermine the serious, unmediated discourse of power and authority. They position themselves in the work through the voices of rogues, clowns, or fools—the literary prototypes of the world of carnival—who decenter the ideological world of other characters. The serio-comical possesses a unique and transforming vitality. Even genres that are only remotely connected with this tradition preserve in themselves the carnivalistic tendency, and this aspect sharply distinguishes them from other genres.

Serio-comical writings share basic characteristics. The first is their new relationship to reality. Their starting point for evaluating and shaping reality is the here-and-now. Unlike other genres, the subject of the serious and at the same time comical representation is presented without what Bakhtin calls "any epic or tragic distance." The action occurs not in the "absolute past of myth and legend" but in the realm of the present day (1984a:108). The second characteristic of the serio-comical genre is related to the first. Instead of relying on legend, serio-comical narratives rely on experience and free invention, and the tone is often critical or cynical. Finally, this innovative genre is multi-styled and hetero-voiced. These authors tend to reject the stylistic rigidity of the formal epic, tragedy, or high rhetoric. They employ in this new genre a multi-tone narration that mixes high and low, serious and comic, elements (1984a:108).

For Bakhtin, the two major genres that constitute the serio-comical realm are the Socratic dialogue and the menippean satire (1984a:106-122). He traces the early history of fiction from antiquity to show how these two ancient art forms continued through the Middle Ages and up to Rabelais. Originally a kind of memoir, the dialogues are characterized by opposition to any official monologism[4] claiming to possess ready-made truth. Early in the stages of development, the genre broke away from the constraints of history, retaining only the Socratic process of dialogically revealing truth within a narrative frame of recorded dialogue. Socratic dialogue was widespread in antiquity. Plato, Xenophon, Antisthenes, Phaedo, Euclid, and others excelled in it, although only the dialogues of Plato and Xenophon have come down to us in non-fragmentary form. For these ancient authors, meaning is the product of a dialogical relationship among speakers.

Despite their intricate, philosophical depth, the dialogues occur in a folk-carnival atmosphere. By using carnival forms,

Socrates freed dialogue from heavy-handed rhetoric, while often focusing on contrasting topics: life and death, darkness and light, winter and summer. The debates are not monologically serious, and the themes defy reduction to singleness of meaning. They often combine the two themes of the pathos of change with the joyful relativity of life. The dialogues are also constructed along the lines of carnival laughter with crownings and decrownings. Socratic dialogue belongs to this serio-comic genre because it derives from carnival debates rather than from absolute rhetorical tactics. Just as carnival is profoundly ambivalent, unresolved, and anti-conventional, Socrates also participates in the carnival mode by refusing to end the dialogue with accepted, unexamined notions.

The Socratic means of seeking truth is counterposed to the naive self-confidence of some people who think they possess certain truths. Socrates, the heroes of his dialogues, and everyone who converses is an ideologist. "The dialogic testing of the idea," Bakhtin writes, "is simultaneously also the testing of the person who represents it" (1984a·111-112). Even the Sophist, the simpleminded who are drawn into dialogue, emerge as ideologists against their will. Indeed, the very events of the dialogues are purely ideological means for seeking and testing truth. Thus, in the Socratic dialogue, ideas are organically linked to the image of essential participants in the dialogue. The embryonic ideas that emerge are treated freely and creatively, and the dialogic nature of thought and expression lies at the base of the Socratic dialogues.

Socratic dialogue gave birth to other genres, including menippean discourse, which is saturated with marketplace elements and whose origins lie in carnivalesque folklore. Menippean discourse takes its name from Menippus of Gadara, a philosopher and cynic of the third century B.C.E. Menippus satirized human follies in combinations of prose and verse. His satires were lost, but the term used to designate the genre, "saturae menippeae," was used in Rome during the first century B.C.E. Within the menippean sphere, the diatribe, soliloquy, and other minor genres of controversy evolved. The Roman author Varro imitated Menippus during the first century B.C.E. Lucian (ca. 120–200 C.E.) also imitated the menippean genre. In various forms, these satires survived through the Middle Ages, the Renaissance, and on into the present. One example of this genre from European literature is Jean Leroy's *Satire Ménippée*, published in 1594, and John Barth's novel *Giles Goat-Boy*, published in 1966, is a modern day example of the menippean genre. But perhaps Lewis Carroll's *Alice's Adventure in Wonderland*, published in 1865, is the most famous example of late menippean style.[5]

The menippean satire, or more simply, the menippea—as pliant and variable as Proteus—also exhibits certain basic characteristics that have implication for our study. These forms are characterized by caricature, parody, and sometimes burlesque, but they are usually less aggressive in tone than other examples of satire. Menippean discourse often ridicules, and is always politically and socially disturbing. It is both tragic and comic (hence the term serio-comical), but less dependent upon history and memoir than the Socratic dialogue. The menippea is free of legend and reflects the verisimilitude of life, and, like the Socratic dialogue, the satires are concerned with "ultimate questions." Fantastic elements and free forms are combined with an emphasis on universalism and a capacity to view the world in broad terms. Authors of this genre are interested in representing the unusual and abnormal states of men and women—what Bakhtin calls the "passions bordering on madness" (1984a:116). Eccentric behavior, inappropriate actions—in short, any kind of behavior that departs from the generally accepted, customary, or established patterns of behavior—are characteristics of the menippea, and the menippea is full of sharp contrasts: virtuous courtesans, generous bandits, ups and downs, transitions and shifts, rises and falls of unexpected and disunited events or persons, and the king who becomes a slave. Other characteristics, which are found in varying degrees of dominance, are parody, the element of laughter and collective gaiety, a plot which is oriented toward a code of improbability, the portrayal of threshold situations (birth and death, for example), the appearance of psychopaths, scandalous actions, but, most importantly, a final utopian, universalistic attitude toward the world. One discovers all these elements, we shall see, in the Esther (M) narrative.

Bakhtin follows the history of carnivalesque literary forms from an early stage in Greek prose romances and ancient menippean satires. He finds parts of the New Testament permeated by menippean carnivalization, including the Gospels, Acts of the Apostles, and the Apocalypse. Among these narrative forms, it is the Gospel account of the "King of the Jews" in particular, entering Jerusalem on a donkey and being given the anticrown crown of thorns, that suggests a radical overturning of authority (Clark and Holquist 1984:250). Roman and Byzantine literature also develop within the orbit of the menippea, and the theme and style of menippean satire represents a counter-tradition to the epic or classical line in European prose. From this point, Bakhtin moves through the big door that Rabelais opened and enters the popular culture of Renaissance folk celebration and on to the modern novel. When compared to Socratic dialogue or menippean satire, the specific weight of the comic element is greatly increased with Rabelais, but Rabelais is part of a common genre tradition which begins in antiquity.

ESTHER RECONSIDERED

One might suggest that a Bakhtinian reading of Esther is a back-reading, methodologically flawed. We will soon discuss Esther in relation to carnival, but it is necessary first to emphasize that the gap between the twentieth-century Bakhtin and the ancient biblical story of Esther is not as wide as it might appear. In this conception, carnival is not to be confused with a kind of celebration that survives with this name today. Instead, folk festivity goes back before the rise of Christianity to the Roman Saturnalia and beyond that to the very primitive communal rituals described by Sir James Frazer. Rituals mingle death and life in a fertility rite (or as Bakhtin calls it, "pregnant death") in the course of which established values and established authority are turned upside down in favor of a "joyous relativity" that signifies the ongoing life of the community.

Bakhtin is quite concerned with questions of *historical* poetics, and herein lies our main justification for a "sidelong glance," as Bakhtin would say, at Esther. Bakhtin's concern in *Rabelais and His World* is with history. Basic links of the carnivalistic generic chain connect Rabelais to a host of writers, ancient and modern. To put it simply, *the carnivalesque is not historically bound to Rabelais or the medieval period*. Rabelais's use of the marketplace, the carnival, and colloquial language developed out of ancient literary art forms. The example of carnival shows us that laughter at its most profound level of meaning emerges from an imaginative world whereby the human community functions through history in a specific way. From the outset, Bakhtin and members of what came to be known as his circle undertook the study of the carnivalesque in its continuous process of generation precisely from the point of view of ideologically meaningful evolution and transformation.

The Hebrew Esther narrative has a kind of stand-alone quality about it. It is the only story of the Hebrew Bible that never mentions God, and it has been described as one of the "most secular" books of the Bible (White 1992:125).[6] Many have dismissed it. In a survey article on the book of Esther, Carey Moore (1992:635) lists the following evaluations:

> I am so hostile to this book [2 Maccabees] and Esther that I could wish that they did not exist at all; for they judaize too greatly and have much pagan impropriety (Martin Luther in "Weimar Ausgabe").

> There is not one noble character in the book. . . . Morally, Est. falls far below the general level of the OT, and even of the Apocrypha (Lewis Paton in the International Critical Commentary on Esther).

> [I] should not be grieved if the Book of Esther were somehow dropped out of Scripture (Samuel Sandmel in *The Enjoyment of Scripture*).

> [The Purim] festival and the book are unworthy of a people which is disposed to bring about its national and moral regeneration under prodigious sacrifice (S. Ben-Chorin in *Kritik des Estherbuches*).

But if the book of Esther is an example of the serio-comical genre, a literary category with roots in antiquity, perhaps these disparaging evaluations need to be reevaluated.

One final note. Rabelais was attacked by the enemies of laughter who granted no special rights to carnival. The Sorbonne condemned his books (though they continued to be distributed and reprinted), and critics have often attempted to cut his work from the canon. Even during his life, Rabelais was violently attacked by the monk du Puits-Herbault and by the Protestant reformer John Calvin. But the voices of these enemies of laughter were eventually drowned out by the voices of the friends of laughter (Bakhtin 1984b:269). The history of Rabelais's reception, a subject to which Bakhtin gives considerable attention in *Rabelais and His World*, is simultaneously the history of misreadings and the history of how the culture of laughter degenerates after reaching its zenith in the Renaissance—a process which is the root cause of such misreadings. If Bakhtin is correct, Rabelais's novel has been so often misunderstood because of a waning carnivalesque consciousness that reduces carnival to debauchery and revelry.

Both Rabelais and the author of the Esther narrative responded to official culture and dogma with carnivalized language, themes, and images. A diminishing carnival perception of the world may explain the futile efforts of a number of interpreters, such as Luther, Paton, Sandmel, Ben-Chorin, and many others who have expressed contempt for the Esther (M) narrative. By overhauling basic views that have so often informed interpreters' artistic and ideological perceptions, a new understanding is possible. This new way of looking at the old story of Esther has implications for the final chapters of the narrative in particular. I will highlight the exceptionally rich imagery of carnival forms, language, and symbols, and attempt to recover the virtually ignored idiom of carnival which is so often obscure to us today.

Proceeding into the largely uncharted territory of the Esther narrative with a Bakhtinian map, I seek to highlight a folk-carnivalistic base by focusing on the book's many carnivalesque images: banquets, the open market, the crown, the mask, "pregnant death," parody, the fool(s), and collective gaiety. It is my purpose to show that the Hebrew Esther narrative derives from folk tradition, complete with ancient ritual and spectacle that characterized saturnalias, carnivals, and the routines of clowns and fools.

But the semiotic theory of the literary carnivalesque developed by Mikhail Bakhtin is more than a mere tool for examining the Esther (M) narrative. The inventory of carnival acts, symbols, and signs derives meaning not only from the profane inversion of canonized values, but even more from the utopian dimension of the story. It is precisely because Haman's desire is real that the celebration at the end carries profound implications.[7] Indeed, the celebration acquires the contours of a worldview

The Hebrew Esther story, quite unlike the Esther (A) and (B) stories and quite unlike much of the material of the Hebrew Bible, originates in (and is to this day a part of) folk culture. It is this folk element that has so often been overlooked. Bakhtin's observation that carnival's crucial scenes often take place on thresholds or platforms and that they occur when a whole lifetime is concentrated in the outcome of a single moment certainly has implication for Esther. Indeed, a carnivalesque spirit permeates this ancient story. In chapters 3–6 I will not attempt to supplant any other reading of Esther, though I will at times contend with the views of other readers. The view of books on a shelf, side by side, is suggestive: each writer contributes to the game called interpretation.

ESTHER
AND THE
CARNIVALESQUE

3

PRELUDE

The Esther (M) story is quite unlike any other narrative of the Hebrew Bible. The following events transpire in this fast-paced drama: The story opens in Susa, the capital of Persia, with the first in a series of complications. In the midst of a lavish banquet, King Ahasuerus (probably to be identified with Xerxes I who reigned from 486 465 B.C.E.)[1] dismisses his wife Vashti for refusing to display herself before the partygoers. The sage Memucan advises the king that the women of Persia will likely be influenced by Queen Vashti and "rebel against the king's officials" and that "there will be no end of contempt and wrath" (1:18). (Unable to think on his own, Ahasuerus almost always seeks or receives unsolicited advice in this story.) Memucan also advises that Vashti never appear again before the king. The king is told that he should "give her royal position to another who is better than she" (1:19). Each beautiful virgin from the land is summoned to Susa, given a lavish cosmetic treatment, and then, finally, ushered to the king's bedchamber when her turn comes to go to the king (2:12). If the king "delight[s] in her" (2:14), she is again summoned by name. Finally, the king chooses Esther who, unbeknown to him, is Jewish and a cousin of Mordecai, an official who serves at the king's gate. The king's vizier (or prime minister), Haman, is promoted above all the officials, and when he becomes incensed at Mordecai for refusing to bow, the vizier gains royal assent to destroy all the Jews of Persia. The date of their destruction is fixed by drawing the lot (pur; 3:7). After receiving advice from Mordecai, Esther decides to beseech the king and thereby save, she hopes, the lives of her people. Through a series of carefully executed plans, she eventually succeeds. Esther exposes Haman in the king's presence as "a foe and enemy" (7:6), and the king, again upon advice, has Haman hanged on the gallows that Haman had prepared for Mordecai. At the end of the story, the Jews celebrate their deliverance on the very month "that had been turned for them from sorrow into gladness" (9:22), and this celebration is called Purim, a name derived from the lots (*purim*). Just before the story ends, Mordecai enjoins the celebrants to keep 14 and 15 Adar "year by year" (9:21) as a holiday whereby the intended victims remember the day they gained relief from their enemies, a day which "had been turned for them . . . from mourning into a holiday" (9:22).

This holiday of celebration and play survives to this day. The story of Esther and Mordecai is read from a special scroll each year, and the mention of Haman's name provokes loud jeering and noise produced by hand-held noisemakers. I wish to examine this plot and holiday of play in greater detail by isolating passages from the Esther (M) story and discussing them in terms of the literary carnivalesque. Throughout, I will look to Bakhtin for theoretical and expositional insight.

THE CARNIVALESQUE: OFFICIAL VS. NON-OFFICIAL CULTURE

Language, semiotics, and historical poetics are three domains of Bakhtin's interests, but another source of his methodology is folk culture. While dividing official and unofficial (or high and low) cultures, he distills their different attitudes with respect to laughter: "A boundless world of humorous forms . . . opposed the official and serious tone of medieval and ecclesiastical and feudal culture" (Clark and Holquist 1984:299-300). And, in another context, Bakhtin writes, "The men [and women] of the Middle Ages participated in two lives: the official and the carnival life. Two aspects of the world, the serious and the laughing aspect, coexisted in their consciousness" (1984b:96). It is an intolerant, one-sided tone of seriousness that distinguishes official medieval culture from the free-jolly atmosphere of folk culture. Laughter, at least the unique form Bakhtin is interested in, was confined to the unofficial sphere of the marketplace. It was foreign to strict forms of social relations and was eliminated from feudal and state ceremonials (Bakhtin 1984b:73). In contrast to the official feast, carnival celebrates temporary liberation from the established order; it removes all hierarchical rank, privileges, and norms. Carnival is the feast of laughter for the folk, and also the feast of change and renewal (Bakhtin 1984b:10). The high spirited democratic laughter of the folk provides an alternative to the official, serious, and rigidly hierarchical structures of the state. Bakhtin's theory of laughter posits an "unofficial folk culture" full of a rebellious spirit of regeneration utterly free from an oppressive dogmatism. (We will return to the themes of laughter and celebration in chapter 6. They will play a major role in establishing the often dismissed Purim festivity as an integral part of this book that belongs to the literary carnivalesque.)

With all its celebration of festive life, carnival asserts itself in radical opposition to official culture. Popular culture, according to Bakhtin, draws swords against and explodes the serious hierarchy and dogmatism that characterizes official culture. In other words, through the carnivalesque game of turning the official world on its head, such action anticipates a new utopian world where hierarchy, authority, and dogma are, to borrow an image from the story of Esther, hanged on the gallows. Bakhtin discovers an interface between a stasis imposed from above and a desire for change from below. In carnival's atmosphere of freedom and celebration, where participants are liberated from serious official culture, a new world order develops where syncretism and differing perspectives are not threatened. The folk of unofficial culture celebrate their freedom from institutionalization; they celebrate the survival and renewal of their spirit over the stifling forces of official order.

Carnivals are celebrations of change originally held on days of feasts in the town square or marketplace, and Bakhtin regards them as the unofficial, "extraecclesiastical and extrapolitical aspect of the world" (1984b:6) that suspends oppressive hierarchical norms of the official world. Carnivals have an other-world-ness quality about them as evidenced by food, drink, blasphemies, and celebrations of the body. Carnival festivity also has an all-inclusive quality about it, and the various actions find their common source in ritual and spectacle elements that are central to the unity of folk culture. Death and life, tears and laughter, and other oppositions form complementary aspects in a world where an unofficial culture celebrates the comic and affirmative.

Carnival's provocative, mirthful inversion of prevailing institutions and their hierarchy also offers an alternative to dogmatism, and in the carnivalesque genre, spaces formerly sanctified diminish in number and importance as they are debased and carnivalized. The action is often predictable: the sacred gives way to the secular, black becomes white, and so forth. In Esther's narrative world the gallows, one symbol of official culture's power, are eventually carnivalized by the king himself: "Hang him [Haman] on that [i.e., on the gallows that Haman had intended for Mordecai]" (7:9). Ahasuerus's golden scepter, another symbol of official culture's authority, will become less prominent and less significant (and is thus carnivalized), by the story's end.[2] Carnival is also a response to the privileged places of official culture, and there are also privileged places in the Esther narrative that are eventually overcome.[3]

In his study of counterculture in *Rabelais and His World*, Bakhtin discovers an experience of ambivalence that is central to life and literature. The ambivalence leads to disruption which is caused by the establishment of both ancient and ever new hierarchies. While he distinguishes between official culture and the culture of laughter in medieval and Renaissance society, Bakhtin repeatedly points to the ancient Socratic dialogue as a prototype of this carnivalesque discourse (1981:24-25, 29, 36-38, 130-31; 1984a:107-15, 120, 122, 140, 143, 156, 164, 178; 1984b:121, 168-69, 286). The lower strata of culture opposes the uniform official high culture in a free-jolly atmosphere that calls attention to the physical side of life while producing a transforming regenerative power. Unofficial culture *must* respond to the rigidly serious, dogmatic culture, and it is this irrepressible, unsilenceable energy issuing from the carnival's alternative appeal—and not so much the particular expressions of folk culture practice—that disrupts institutionalized culture.

This carnival perception of the world has roots in antiquity, and one finds some evidence to support his claim in the old Esther (M) story. Mordecai expresses this inevitable impulse when he says to Esther, "For if you keep silence at such a time as this, relief and deliverance will rise for the Jews from another quarter" (4:14a), and even though plot details suggest just the opposite, Haman's wife, Zeresh, will later tell her husband that his fate is sealed: "If Mordecai before whom your downfall has begun, is of the Jewish people, you will not prevail against him, but will surely fall before him" (6:13b). Carnival gives literature a solution to the problems posed by rigid and authoritarian official culture of the ancient *and* medieval worlds, much as parties serve more recent novelists, such as F. Scott Fitzgerald, in exposing the fragmentation of contemporary secular society.

For Bakhtin, the primary manifestation of humorous medieval folk culture was in ritual spectacles and comic verbal compositions. Humorous forms manifest themselves in carnivalesque literature in different ways—as open air spectacles, parodies (especially of religious rituals), and in various forms of billingsgate, curses, and oaths. The eccentric behavior of carnival, like the eccentric behavior of Purim, is a ritualized mocking of customary official existence, and folk culture's most important celebratory act is by far the unique act of carnival itself.

> Thus, the unofficial folk culture of the Middle Ages and even of the Renaissance had its own territory and its own particular time, the time of fairs and feasts. This territory, as we have said, was a peculiar second world within the official medieval order and was ruled by a special type of relationship, a free, familiar, marketplace relationship. Officially the palaces, churches, institutions, and private homes were dominated by hierarchy and etiquette, but in the marketplace a special kind of speech was heard, almost a language of its own, quite unlike the language of Church, palace, courts, and institutions. It was also unlike the tongue of official literature or of the ruling classes. . . . The festive marketplace combined many genres and forms, all filled with the same unofficial spirit (Bakhtin 1984b:154).

When he turns his attention to dialogue, Bakhtin conceives it in opposition to "the authoritarian word," in a fashion reminiscent of folk culture's opposition to an official culture: "Devoid of any zones of cooperation with other types of words, the 'authoritarian word' thus excludes dialogue. Similarly, any official culture that considers itself the only respectable model dismisses all other cultural strata as invalid or harmful" (Bakhtin 1984b:x). But the language of carnival overcomes "the authoritarian word." Marketplace language is an "absolutely gay and fearless talk, free and frank, which echoes in the festive square beyond all verbal prohibitions, limitations, and conventions" (Bakhtin 1984b:167). Just as "the authoritarian word" does not allow any other speech that would interfere with it, so official culture attempts to constrain unofficial culture. The authoritarian word in Esther is "the law," and carnival transgresses such laws. Indeed, carnival is anti-law.[4]

ESTHER AND OFFICIAL VS. NON-OFFICIAL CULTURE

What may now strike us as we enter Esther's narrative world is the presence of two cultures, one official and one unofficial in Bakhtin's parlance, one bearing down on the other in large part because of one peevish, sordid, and vile man. The official culture is led by the king's vizier and supported by the king himself, and Esther and Mordecai are the chief representatives of the unofficial culture. Several passages in the story reveal these two distinct cultures. The first image of one such culture is found at the very beginning:

> This happened in the days of Ahasuerus, the same Ahasuerus who ruled over one hundred twenty-seven provinces from India to Ethiopia. In those days when King Ahasuerus sat on his royal throne in the citadel of Susa, in the third year of his reign, he gave a banquet for all his officials and ministers (1:1-3a).

An opening scene is always important to consider because it sets a tone for the entire narrative. The narrator launches this story with a description of things that happened "in the days of Ahasuerus" (v. 1), a temporal reference that looks back to a distant past and gives the appearance of a story told from a history-like point of view. A similar phrase in the next verse, "in those days," reminds the reader of this perspective. This near duplication of words in the first two verses is necessary because of the long, and in the Hebrew unusually long, parenthetical expression of v. 1 that reveals the dimensions of Ahasuerus's rule: he commands one hundred twenty-seven provinces, all the way from India to Ethiopia. This opening scene also highlights important events and adumbrates a number of themes that will be developed throughout the unfolding story. The king loses face when Vashti refuses to become his pawn (v. 12), and upon recommendation of the sages, Vashti is banished. Consequently, the Persian throne becomes vacant, thus providing an opportunity for Esther's enthronement.

From the outset, the reader gains important information with respect to this royal Persian worldview. We imagine a king showing off "the great wealth of his kingdom and the splendor and pomp of his majesty for many days" (v. 4). He sits on his "royal throne" (v. 2), which is literally "the seat of his kingdom." The image may suggest either that he is firmly in power or perhaps the author implies that it is in Susa, one of the four Persian capitals, where the king happens now to be dwelling and ruling. The story moves quickly from imperial pomp to the much more narrow and absurd aspect of domestic life. All women throughout the kingdom will soon be commanded to give honor to their husbands. This law, a "royal order" (v. 19), becomes effective when letters are sent to all the "royal provinces" (v. 22). As Ahasuerus prepares to shop for a new wife, Esther is brought to his "royal palace," and when she wins his favor he sets the "royal crown" upon her head (2:16-17). Then at her coronation banquet, the king gives gifts with "royal liberality" (2:18). After Esther becomes queen, Mordecai refers to her "royal dignity" (4:14). Esther puts on her "royal robes" just before she is summoned by the king who sits, once again, on his "royal throne" (5:1), and in chapter 6 Haman reveals his desire to wear the "royal robes" and "royal crown" (v. 8). The pomp is never ending.

Much attention is also given to dimensions in the first chapter. A hyperbolic tone is suggested by the reference to the one hundred twenty-seven *medinot*, which must here be translated as "provinces"—not satrapy, the standard administrative unit in Persia.[5] If the *medinot* are regions within the satrapy, i.e., if they are provinces, we may conjecture that the author avoids the standard designation in order to present a higher number. The length of two of the banquets is also mentioned in the first chapter. This pompous display of wealth and power lasts for one hundred and eighty days (v. 4). The phrase, "many days" of v. 4 in Esther (M) is not found in Esther (A) or (B) and reinforces the idea that the Hebrew story reflects a hyperbolic tone, a characteristic tone of carnival writings. The banquet mentioned in v. 5 is given for all, "both great and small," a phrase also not found in the Esther (B) narrative (Moore 1971: 7).[6] At the end of Ahasuerus's second banquet, the king orders "each one" to do as he or she pleases. This repetition—the phrase is literally "person and person"—provides emphasis and is characteristic of the author's style (1:22; 2:11; 3:4, 14; 8:9).

The opening scene thus sets the stage for a drama of world history and world politics. On this vast stage, another crisis will develop around the action and inaction of two individuals: Haman, armed with power and a high ranking member of the official culture, and Mordecai, a man from the unofficial culture, who refuses to give Haman obeisance, even though the king had commanded it (3:2).

An Official Culture

The Persians at the court are members of the official culture in this story, and the author invests much to accentuate the official nature of Ahasuerus's palace. Officials are everywhere in this story, and they're fond of acting in an official capacity. The king, vizier, satraps, governors, and princes have responsibilities throughout the empire (1:1; 3:1, 12; 8:9; 9:3; cf. Clines 1984: 46). Even at the syntactic level, the author uses language that reflects what Michael Fox calls a "courtly, somewhat stiff character" (1991:13). Banquets (discussed below) are a way of life, and it is in the midst of these feasts that the author also calls attention to the official nature of life at the Persian court.

The author emphasizes the king's official authority. His servants attend him during the day (chap. 1) as well as at night (6:1, 3). The chief eunuch has the responsibility of preparing for the king's pleasure. We witness the extent of the king's rule when he summons "all the beautiful virgins" to see which one "pleases" him the most (2:3-4), and this motif of "coming before the king" appears throughout. Vashti is never again to "come before" King Ahasuerus (1:19). His command is for all the beautiful virgins in the empire to be brought into the care of Hegai, and 2:14 makes it clear that the women could appear before the king only when summoned by name. At 4:11, Esther emphasizes that no one can step inside the king's inner court unsummoned. The penalty for violating this law is death. Esther reveals that she has "not been called to come in to the king for thirty days," a reference no doubt to the king's practice of summoning a woman for sex. Bowing down, summoning all virgins of the empire, making laws on a whim—all these images leave little doubt that this is an oppressively regulated atmosphere.

An Official Culture's "Laws"

The Persian court's official nature is also suggested by frequent reference to laws, both in the opening scene and throughout the book. The word "law" appears often in Esther and always denotes official royal decisions.[7] The law of the Persians affects all aspects of life. That servants must follow the letter of the law is hardly surprising, but even their serving of wine is the subject of a royal edict (1:8), and the authority of men in their houses throughout the empire is also set by decree (1:20-22). Illegal actions are punishable by law (4:11), and imperial edicts allow genocide (3:10-14). This is a world where the king's wishes instantly become reality by means of an oppressive legal machinery. In this multiracial world (1:1, 22, 3:8, 12; 8:9; 9:30), the laws convey an impression of stability, but the monarch will find himself caught in a web of his own law when Esther pleads before him "to revoke" Haman's letter authorizing genocide. The king does grant Esther and Mordecai permission to write a law as they please on this issue, but also tells them that "an edict [such as Haman's] written in the name of the king and sealed with the king's ring cannot be revoked" (8:8).[8]

Queen Vashti becomes the object of a royal edict after she

refuses to bow to her husband's wishes (1:13-21), and when he becomes enraged he responds to her "according to the law" (1:15). (In the Hebrew the phrase is emphasized by its unusual syntactical arrangement.) In an effort to resolve the situation, the king consults his advisers knowledgeable in the law. These so-called wise men are the ones who know the laws and are able to suggest legal actions the king might take against Vashti. They suggest that she be banished (lit. that she "never again [be allowed] to come before" the king [1:19]), and the *unnecessary* mention of the king's law reminds us of its presence and unalterable quality in 1:19-20. When his anger against his wife subsides, Ahasuerus thinks of her again and remembers her in terms of what "had been decreed against her" (2:1). By responding according to law, Ahasuerus acts in measured, calculated, that is, in good official fashion. Indeed, no aspect of Persian life escapes the rule of law. The empire is governed strictly according to imperial law, which is mentioned at virtually every turn of the plot, and the threat of genocide is compounded by the unalterable law (1:19; 8:8).

The king's response to Vashti's action in chapter 1 is not the only instance where official, royal laws play a major part in plot development. Individual and community responses to the law will become important issues in this story, and they often have a lingering effect. Just after Haman requests permission for a decree calling for the destruction of the Jews, the secretaries write a letter, according to "all that Haman commanded" (3:12). The letter contains a command to all the regional officers who are charged to inform the people of its content. Like all Persian laws, this edict is addressed to the satraps, the governors, and all the people of the provinces in the script and language of each. A tremendous administrative apparatus goes into action to make sure that the word spreads to everyone.

At 4:11, Persian law is an issue once again. Mordecai and Esther attempt to cancel Haman's edict. When Mordecai learns of the genocidal plan, he sends Hathach to Esther with the written decree (that calls for the destruction of the Jews) and a verbal message to go before the king in supplication for the people. After receiving these words from Hathach, Esther responds by telling him to return to Mordecai with her message: Initiating conversation with the king is risky business because, according to the law, no man or woman can enter the king's inner court unless they are summoned. The penalty for violating this law is death. But this law contains an escape clause: the king reserves the right to erase the infraction by extending his nice, shiny, golden scepter.[9] Some Persian laws have built-in escape clauses; others do not. Mordecai, Esther, and in fact all the Jews of the land, have no chance for escape—or so it appears—because no such clause exists that would cancel the pogrom edict. At 8:8, the moment when the decree bringing deliverance to the Jews is authorized, the motif of unalterable law surfaces again. In a scene that obviously parallels the original pogrom writing edict of 3:10-15a, the king grants Mordecai and Esther the privilege of writing as they please in the name of the king (8:8-14). Mordecai writes to the one hundred twenty-seven provinces and also to the Jews in their language (8:9). Even though they can write as they please, and even with Haman dead, the law calling for annihilation still threatens the Jews throughout the kingdom because no one has the authority to revoke Haman's previous edict against the Jews. However, Esther and Mordecai, in conjunction with Ahasuerus, do take steps to "reverse the irreversible" (Clines 1984:19), and this response action is carried out according to law (8:13, 14, 17; 9:1, 13, 14).

An Emerging Unofficial Culture

If Ahasuerus, ruler of the one hundred twenty-seven provinces, and Haman, his right hand man, epitomize official culture, Esther and Mordecai are certainly contrasting members in this society. Much is at stake here as the unofficial culture tries to cancel official unalterable laws. Ahasuerus promotes Haman and places his seat above all the other officials (3:1). The king also commands that all servants at the king's gate must bow to Haman. Just after Mordecai refuses to bow to Haman, Haman informs the king that a "certain people" do not keep the king's laws (3:8). Haman then asks him for a decree of destruction.

This "certain people," as Haman labels them, lives in the Persian kingdom, and they have their own laws, laws which, according to the incensed Haman, are "different from those of every other people." It is in fact the laws of this unofficial culture that, at least from Haman's perspective in the presence of Ahasuerus, prevent them from "keep[ing] the king's laws" (3:8). It's a simple case of conflicting laws—or so Haman would have the easily persuadable Ahasuerus believe. Of course, Haman's problem is a personal one; he's incensed because Mordecai will not bow down to *him* (3:5-6). Haman plans to kill Mordecai because Mordecai costs Haman the enjoyment of his office, and, in order to accomplish his goal, Haman asks the king to issue a decree calling for the destruction of *all* Jews. In other words, by means of an official law, the unofficial laws and the unofficial culture of the land will be destroyed, killed, and annihilated (3:13; cf. 7:4). Such threats to official Persian law will not be tolerated in the Persian court. After learning of this unofficial culture's laws and the alleged threat they pose, the king gives Haman the royal ring, and, along with it, the power to issue official documents and decrees. (While Ahasuerus gives Haman explicit instructions to "do with them as it seems good to you" in 3:11, it appears that Haman does not have full power. In 6:4 he must ask permission to execute Mordecai before the pogrom.) This non-official culture finds itself close to annihilation as Haman works to prove himself "the enemy of the Jews," an epithet assigned explicitly by the narrator at 3:10 and 8:1, and with variation by Esther at 7:6.

Thus Haman receives permission to deal with people whom he finds offensive, or, more accurately, Haman, offended by *one* man, receives permission to kill *all* the Jews of the land. In 3:12, the king's secretaries are summoned. They write to the king's satraps and governors over all the provinces to every province in its own script and language.[10] The scribes dutifully record Haman's edict as Haman directs them. This edict is written in the king's name and sealed with the royal signet ring, and is promulgated throughout the land. In addition, the letter is translated into the language and script of every people. Such exaggeration makes the point that the unofficial culture, namely, the threatened Jews, stand little chance to overturn an official edict such as this. The official orders are "to destroy, to kill, and to annihilate all Jews" (v. 13; Esther, a member of the unofficial culture, will use these same three verbal forms in 7:4.[11]) The edict is chilling. To the phrase "all Jews" is added the more explicit (and perhaps unnecessary) description of "young and old," "women and children." Considerable attention is given to the official nature of this action. This edict is written in the name of the king and sealed with the king's ring (3:12). The letters are sent to every province by proclamation calling on all the people to be ready for that day. In v. 15, "the couriers went quickly by order of the king."

There is a long delay between the dispatch of Haman's decree and its execution: The couriers make haste, although Adar is eleven months away (Fox 1991:54), and this movement contrasts with the leisurely paced action in the opening scene (1:1-12). Much attention is given to the comprehensive, fast-paced nature of Haman's actions: the secretaries write according to "all" that Haman commands; the letters go to "all the provinces" and to "all the peoples" in "every province;" couriers take the letters to "all the king's provinces;" the decree is for "every province;" and "all the people" are to prepare for the pogrom (3:12-14). 13 Adar is the day designated for genocide, and Ahasuerus will later remind Esther that imperial laws are unalterable (8:8). Official culture bears down on unofficial cultures as we observe a shift from gender violence to ethnic violence: One woman is banished; all women become subject to their husbands; all virgins are summoned only to be followed by the news that all Jews will die because of the evil plan of one demonic man. This is the fate for all in the unofficial realm who suffer under official laws of the land. These scenes of gender and ethnic violence end with a description of the king and Haman sitting down to drink as the "city of Susa [is] thrown into confusion" (3:15). How can non-official, powerless culture respond? Esther holds the key.

THE CARNIVALESQUE AND BANQUETS

There is an ancient tie between the feast and the spoken word.
—Bakhtin, *Rabelais and His World*

For Bakhtin, the most important writer of the carnivalesque is the sixteenth-century writer, François Rabelais. The sharing of food is an important element in most carnivalesque writings, and banquet images play a major role in his novel, *Gargantua and Pantagruel.*[12] Images of food and drink appear on virtually every page of *Gargantua* as metaphors, as epithets, and as major elements in plot sequences: "Almost all the themes of the novel come about through it; hardly an episode could manage without it. The most varied objects and phenomena of the world are brought into direct contact with food and drink—including the most lofty and spiritual things" (Bakhtin 1981:178). A hyperbolic tone permeates the entire novel. Gargantua is born on a day of feasting. His father "ordered meat by the ton, wine by the thousand gallons. No pains were spared to honor his guests." Everyone is "ever ready to eat salted meat, which serves to rouse the thirst." During the banquet, his mother overeats on tripe. Then Gargantua is born, shouting "Drink, drink, drink," and is immediately "wined" (Rabelais 1936:12, 15, 23, 24). The eating and drinking series is often narrated with great detail, and the images of food and drink are sometimes intertwined with religious concepts and symbols, such as prayers, papal directives, altars, and so forth.

Banquets serve to bring people together, and those who come to the feast come not just to consume enormous quantities of food. In a chapter titled "Banquet Imagery in Rabelais," Bakhtin concludes the discussion by noting that

> banquet images in the popular-festive tradition (and in Rabelais) differ sharply from the images of private eating or private gluttony and drunkenness in early bourgeois literature. The latter express the contentment and satiety of the selfish individual, his [or her] personal enjoyment, and not the triumph of the people as a whole. Such imagery is torn away from the process of labor and struggle; it is removed from the marketplace and is confined to the house and the private chamber (abundance in the home); it is no longer the "banquet for all

the world," in which all take part, but an intimate feast with hungry beggars at the door (1984b:301-302).

Just as the carnivalesque crowd is not merely another throng, the feast is not simply another meal. With its crowds and abundance of food, the carnival feast is not for mere idlers and gluttons, men and women who are habitually at table. It is rather "a primary, indestructible ingredient of human civilization; it may become sterile and even degenerate, but it cannot vanish" (1984b:276). The unique aspect of carnival festivity arises, therefore, from its communal nature and its difference from everyday life, a difference that participants demonstrate and celebrate through unconventional behavior. Guests leave behind particular worries and cares from the official world and don a celebrative mask as they enter the feast. The people are "organized in their own way, . . . outside of and contrary to all existing forms of the coercive socioeconomic and political organization, which is suspended for the time of the festivity" (Bakhtin 1984b:255; original emphasis).

In carnival, change and crisis, ridicule and laughter replace dogma and authority. The spectacle staged by banquet rituals is not actually directed against institutions or authority figures, whose functions are only temporarily usurped, but rather against the loss of a utopian potential brought about by authority and hegemony. The feast, which is not anti-work or anti-production, produces only itself and releases such a utopian potential. Bakhtin does not describe the feast in terms of practical conditions of a community at work, or in terms of the physiological need for food. Instead, the feast has "an essential, meaningful philosophical content" (1984b:8).

Early in *Rabelais and His World*, Bakhtin differentiates between official feasts and the carnivalesque banquets. The ecclesiastic, feudal, or state-sponsored official feasts of the Middle Ages and Renaissance had no regenerative power and they did not lead people out of any existing world order. They only sanctioned and reinforced the status quo. These official feasts intensified all that was "stable, unchanging, perennial," and lacked the spirit of laughter. They were "monolithically serious" (1984b:9).

Bakhtin demonstrates once again his interest in historical poetics when discussing banquets: "Through *all the stages of historic development* feasts were linked to moments of crisis, of breaking points in the cycle of nature or in the life of society" (1984b:9; emphasis added). This festive spirit shows up first in antiquity. While Bakhtin's interest lies with feasts of the Middle Ages, he traces the phenomenological significance of food back to its primitive roots, that is, to the conclusion of the hunt:

> [Our] awakening consciousness could not but concentrate on this moment, could not help borrowing from it a number of substantial images determining [the feast's] interrelation with the world. [Our] encounter with the world in the act of eating is joyful, triumphant; [we] triumph over the world, devour it without being devoured [ourselves] (1984b:281).

During the Middle Ages, the church assimilated popular festivals into the Christian calendar. Even the flamboyant "carnival" became part of the pre-Lenten festivity. Shortly after the Middle Ages festivities became less centered on the church, and were sometimes replaced by parties.

ESTHER AND BANQUETS

The stories of Esther and *Gargantua and Pantagruel* are separated by almost two millennia, but the series of eating, drinking, and drunkenness (and other shared elements mentioned above) plays an enormous role in both narratives. Images of banqueting and drinking appear frequently in the book of Esther. The key words ("banqueting" and "drinking") are both translations of a form of the Hebrew word *shatah* ("drink"), and virtually half of the occurrences of *mishteh* ("banquet" or "feast") in the Bible are found in the comparatively short book of Esther.[13] Since this saturation of food and drink motifs is common in the literary carnivalesque, we may explore the intertextual characteristics of this feasting in the Esther narrative. These banquets have important thematic and intertextual significance because they call our attention to the transfer of power, and we will discover that banquet scenes in Esther tend toward one of two varieties: the official and unofficial types. As the story opens, banqueting is little more than a garish display of luxury and opulence for those who hold power. But things change.

Early Banquets

The first hint that the Esther narrative is part of the literary carnivalesque tradition is found at the beginning of the story. The first half of the first chapter contains references and descriptions of three distinct banquets: Ahasuerus's banquet for the nobility (1:2-4), Ahasuerus's banquet for the men of Susa (1:5-8), and Vashti's banquet for the women (1:9). Ahasuerus will arrange for yet another banquet in 2:18 when Esther is enthroned. Banqueting must have been a favorite pastime at this Persian court.

An important issue to consider, as power is transferred in this story, is who calls or arranges the banquets. In the opening scenes, the king arranges three (1:3; 1:5; 2:18), and Vashti one (1:9). These first banquets are, therefore, official court banquets, and they (unlike those that follow) provide a means for conspicuous displays of wealth and power. Official culture seizes the opportunity to show off its "greatness," or even to celebrate after an edict is issued calling for the destruction of the Jews (3:15). From this point on, official culture will assume less responsibility for calling or arranging the banquets.[14]

During the first banquet (1:2-4), for half a year, Ahasuerus flaunts his wealth. The official tone is highlighted by the report of those in attendance: "all his officials and ministers," "the army," and "the nobles and governors" throughout the land. The second banquet (1:5-8), though limited to the inhabitants of Susa, is once again for "all officials." The king commands the guests "to do as each one desires," and the drinking is "by flagons, without restraint" (1:8). While it lasts a mere seven days, the author provides more details of this feast. Given the Hebrew Bible's laconic style, the attention to scenery is quite unusual, and this expansive description provides the reader a rare glimpse of palace life. Notice the opulence and extravagance.

> There were white cotton curtains and blue hangings tied with cords of fine linen and purple to silver rings and marble pillars. There were couches of gold and silver on a mosaic

pavement of porphyry, marble, mother-of-pearl, and colored stones. Drinks were served in golden goblets, goblets of different kinds, and the royal wine was lavished according to the bounty of the king. Drinking was by flagons, without restraint; for the king had given orders to all the officials of his palace to do as each one desired (1:6-8).

This second feast has another claim to notice, namely at the level of plot. It is at the end of this banquet, on the seventh day, that Queen Vashti is deposed after refusing to display her beauty for all. The subsequent events of the story are all related to Vashti's refusal to cater to her husband's whims, to the throne from which she is deposed, and to her successor. Vashti's banquet, the third in the opening chapter, is confined in narrative space to only one sentence, but two important motifs are introduced: segregation (in this case of the sexes) and the queen's banquet. Both of these motifs will appear later in the story: The Jews will soon be singled out (3:8-15a), and Esther will give her own banquets just after she becomes queen (5:4-8; 7:1-9). Finally, the king sponsors a banquet—the fourth in the series—for his officers and servants in honor of Esther's coronation. This feast might appear to be for the sole purpose of honoring Esther, but the sequence of events suggests that Ahasuerus is, once again, simply in the festive mood. With his former party-spoiling wife out of the picture and with the one who is "admired by all who saw her" his, he's ready to celebrate (2:15-18). He demonstrates his generous, not to mention capricious and chauvinistic, impulses once more by now granting tax relief (or relief from forced labor).[15]

Middle Banquets

Like the banquets of the opening scenes, the middle banquets are united by a single common feature: These *mishteh* provide Haman and Ahasuerus an opportunity to eat and drink together. The king and his right hand man celebrate at 3:15; 5:4-8; and 7:1-2. These scenes, taken together, serve as a foil to the first series of banquets. While the opening feasts are marked by opulence and pomposity, the middle feasts are marked by curiosity and suspense. Will Haman get his way? What does Esther have in mind at the banquets she prepares? What are the implications of her fasting (and her people's fasting) as she prepares a banquet for a man who is planning to kill her and her people? Can we expect her fate to be any different from the one that Vashti has already suffered?

In 3:15, Haman and Ahasuerus "sit down to drink." They agree to the terms of "destroying, killing and annihilating" a whole people, and, after the administrative machinery has been turned on, they celebrate their agreement over drinks. The author presents a picture of sharp contrasts. With the couriers "hurrying themselves" and the city in a state of confusion, the king and Haman sit down for a leisurely Neroesque drink. Just after Haman celebrates with the king, the Jews of the empire begin to fast (4:3) as they learn of the planned pogrom. Fasting—a noteworthy counterpart to feasting—will appear again. Esther asks the Jews of Susa to fast with her and with her maidservants in 4:16, just before she prepares a banquet for Haman and Ahasuerus. The difference in the two cultures, one official and the other unofficial in Bakhtin's parlance, is accentuated by the Persians in the court who feast, and the Jews, outside the palace, who mourn and fast after the royal decree is issued. This fasting stands in stark contrast to the royal banquets in the book, but the instrument of change will move from Jewish fast to Jewish feast. Communal fasts will be transformed by the story's end into communal feasts, that is, the feasts of Purim.

Esther sponsors her first banquet in 5:4-8 and her second in 7:1-9. These two feasts also feature Haman and Ahasuerus, but with an interesting change: Esther prepares the meals. Esther is certainly in no party mood. In fact, it is hungry Esther who is now preparing banquets for the man who has laid plans to take her life and the lives of her people. Instead of interceding for her people, Esther invites the king and her enemy, Haman, to dinner. The scenes highlight the delicate nature of the bargaining as Esther seeks to achieve her goal. Maybe she suspects— and by now we certainly do—that this king so fond of drink may be more likely to grant her request over wine. She makes her preliminary request by inviting the king and Haman to a banquet at the end of her three day fast (4:16-5:4). Her prominence is suggested by Ahasuerus, who responds to her request by quickly ordering Haman to be brought in according to Esther's word (5:5). It is literally at this "banquet of wine" that the king issues his generous command: "What is your petition? It shall be granted you. And what is your request? Even to the half of my kingdom, it shall be fulfilled" (5:6). Ahasuerus obviously enjoys his right to dispense such half-the-kingdom favors, for he speaks these same words before and after this scene (5:3 and 7:2). Esther prolongs the suspense by inviting the king and Haman to yet another banquet on the following day. She tells the king that she will reveal her wish at that time. Revealing her opposition to the king's right hand man as well as revealing her ethnic and religious origins were, of course, serious matters— even to a king who makes sweeping promises. Haman leaves Esther's banquet "happy and in good spirits" (5:9), and, in preparation for the next day's banquet, is advised by his wife to go to the (next) banquet in "good spirits" (5:14). Thus these two feasts provide the author an opportunity to reveal the inner life of characters, an important feature of biblical Hebrew narrative (Craig 1993:124-43).

After another round of preliminaries, Ahasuerus repeats his half-the-kingdom offer in 7:2. Esther responds, finally revealing her petition: "Let my life be given me . . . and the lives of my people . . . for we have been sold, I and my people, to be destroyed, to be killed, and to be annihilated" (7:3-4). Esther's choice of words—to be "destroyed," "killed," and "annihilated"—match those that the king's secretaries recorded in the edict against the Jews (3:13), and they now ring in Haman's ears. Esther does not reveal the enemy's name, but allows Ahasuerus to draw it out of her: "Who is he, and where is he, who has presumed to do this?" (7:5). It's dangerous for Esther to speak this way. She makes her request and also offers a confession. Esther acknowledges that she is a Jew, and she reveals that she is united with her people.

Esther's banquets serve a very different function from the opening banquets. The landscape of power and authority is beginning to change. Haman is falling, quite literally in 7:8 (*naphal*); Esther is rising. Non-official culture, represented here by

Esther (5:1-8 and 7:1-6) and Mordecai (4:13-14), uses feasts as a tool for gaining power.

Final Banquets

The author mentions three banquets in the final chapters of the book: the Jews celebrate Mordecai's new position with a banquet (8:17), the first feast of Purim is celebrated on 14 Adar (9:17, 19), and the second feast of Purim is celebrated on 15 Adar (9:18). Unlike the initial and middle banquets, the feasts at the end are celebratory and are for the Jews exclusively (i.e., they are "non-official" in nature). The final feasts are a symbol of life celebrated in the presence of death. So often dismissed as late, extraneous additions to the story, they are in fact an essential component of this early carnivalesque genre. Far from being incidental or late, and hence non-essential elements of the plot sequence, these final banquets are a fitting conclusion in this type of story.[16]

These final banquets are linked by a common image—just as the early and middle banquets were—of communal solidarity. After Esther is given Haman's house, after Haman is hanged on the gallows, and after Mordecai receives the "royal robes of blue and white, with a great golden crown and a mantle of fine linen and purple" (8:15a), the narrator reveals that "the city of Susa shouted and rejoiced" (8:15b). It is at this point that we learn there was "gladness and joy among the Jews, a festival and a holiday" (8:17). The transformation from Haman and Ahasuerus's drinking party at 3:15, where "the city of Susa was thrown into confusion," is obvious. So is the change from chapter 1 where feasting was no more than an opulent display of wealth and power. The Jews now rejoice and celebrate with a festival and a holiday because of the decree allowing self-defense. While the threat of numerous enemies is still real (8:3), unofficial culture appears to understand Esther and Mordecai's triumph over Haman as a sign that they will be victorious.

The Purim feasts, celebrated on two separate days (9:17, 19 and 9:18), commemorate the reversal of the expected fate of the Jews. The celebration is sparked by Haman's loss of power—the one who is prototypically the enemy of the Jews—and they are also the symbol par excellence of the Jews' empowerment. These are unofficial culture's celebratory feasts which parallel the banquets of the opening chapter. But the author also suggests some differences. Provincial Jews celebrate the holiday on 14 Adar, and Jews in Susa celebrate on 15 Adar. The 14 Adar feast, like the king's first banquet in 1:2-4, includes residents from the various provinces; the second feast, on 15 Adar, like the king's banquet of 1:5-8, is limited to the residents of Susa. This parallel may remind the reader of the opening imperial mood, but unlike at the beginning, the participants now have *reason* to celebrate. The Purim custom includes the sending of food to fellow Jews, but, again in contrast to the opening scene, this festivity is to be observed each year, even by future generations (9:21, 23, 27, 28). The one "day of feasting" in and outside Susa is mentioned three times in a small narrative space (9:17-19). Ahasuerus threw a party for one hundred and eighty days (1:4), but the one day Purim banquets will endure.

The frequent reference to food and drink in the story of Esther, therefore, takes on special significance when we consider Bakhtin's comments on the importance of carnivalesque feasts:

> The feast is always essentially related to time . . . Moreover, through all the stages of historic development feasts were linked to moments of crisis, of breaking points in the cycle of nature or in the life of society . . . Moments of death and revival, of change and renewal always led to a festive perception of the world (1984b:9).

Such communion of shared drinking and eating, from ancient to modern times, is a celebration of life by communities united against the darkness of night.

THE CARNIVALESQUE
AND THE OPEN MARKET/SQUARE

> In carnivalized literature the square, as a setting for the action of the plot, becomes two-leveled and ambivalent: it is as if there glimmered through the actual square the carnival square of free familiar contact and communal performances of crowning and decrowning.
> —Mikhail Bakhtin, *Problems of Dostoevsky's Poetics*

The main arena for carnival acts is the public square and the streets adjoining it. The square is a place of openness and play outside the scrutiny of the church, the direct concern of the crown, or any force that threatens the folk, and state or official culture—whatever form it might take—is always located beyond the square. At once public yet not official, concerned with a range of social identities distinct from those imposed by the state or official society, the square presents a specific social profile. The square Bakhtin has in mind is that of the common people or unofficial culture. It is here that bazaars, theaters, and taverns in the European tradition of the thirteen, fourteenth and subsequent centuries are located.

Bakhtin isolates certain authors who discover in open spaces possibilities for "exteriorization" (1981:136). It is Rabelais's "extraordinary *spatial and temporal expanses* that leap at us from the pages of [his] novel" (Bakhtin 1981:167; original emphasis). The marketplace becomes for him and other writers of the carnivalesque the center of all that is unofficial. It is the place opposed to all official order and official ideology. It is the place where people come to meet and intermingle, and in different kinds of public life there are different kinds of public spaces. The carnival square is not equivalent to what might be called the civic spaces of government life where individuals speak as citizens of the state and thus enter history through state membership, and the actions in carnival stories are not yet concentrated in rooms of private family life. The plot takes in various countries and unfolds for everyone to see under the open sky—in battles, journeys, or global movement.

The marketplace of the Renaissance is a world all its own, a world where performances such as loud cursings, profanities, oaths and organized shows are imbued with an atmosphere of "freedom, frankness, and familiarity" (Bakhtin 1984b:153). Carnival life is constituted by the public square, the place where the rogue, clown, and fool congregate. They lay life bare and shape it. These figures of the rogue, clown, fool, and all they represent are connected to this place where members of unofficial society congregate. These three figures play a vital role in the public square setting (Bakhtin 1981:159).

In a grand sweep of history, Bakhtin himself provides justification for linking the Esther narrative to the carnivalesque. The folk on the carnival square display a specific historical character: "the body of the people on a market square during carnival is first of all aware of its unity in time" (1984b:255). They are not just there celebrating or escaping the shackles of coercive socioeconomic and political forces. On the contrary, they are aware of the uniqueness of their location in space and time:

> [They] are conscious of [their] uninterrupted continuity within time, of [their] relative historic immortality. . . . The people do not perceive a static image of their unity . . . but instead the uninterrupted continuity of their becoming and growth, of the unfinished metamorphosis of death and renewal (1984b:255-56).

But what does the public square and the streets adjoining it have to do with the Esther (M) story?

ESTHER AND THE OPEN MARKET/SQUARE

Every day Mordecai would walk around in front of the court of the harem, to learn how Esther was and how she fared.
—Esth 2:11

One feature of the literary carnivalesque is the image of official society located beyond the square, beyond the place where the folk reside, and the book of Esther, an example of early carnivalesque literature, displays a division between insiders and outsiders. When we turn to this story, we discover not only that official and unofficial cultures reside in two different locations, but that unofficial culture often finds itself outside in open spaces.[17] The author provides a number of spatial coordinates which allow the reader (or hearer) to visualize the action that takes place. What the images suggest in their entirety is a concentric circle of power, with the king at the very center. It is Ahasuerus who holds power in this story and who has the privilege of sharing it. Esther, Mordecai, and Haman will all approach the king at various moments in this story, and the king will elevate all three to high positions in his court. Initially, Esther and Mordecai are situated away from the king. They will have opportunities of coming into his presence, but they must work around the safeguards that are intended to protect the king. In the sections that follow, we will consider two images related to space in the Esther (M) narrative: a) open areas and b) movement to and from the king, a man at the center of power.

The author distinguishes the *birah*, "acropolis" or "citadel" in this book, from the city itself (3:15; 4:1; 4:6; 8:15; cf. Berg 1979:49, n. 5). Situated outside the major players who reside in the acropolis or citadel are those who live in the city of Susa and, beyond them, others who live in the outlying provinces. At times it is necessary for edicts to be transferred from the center of power to the outer limits of this concentric pattern. Outsiders, Esther and Mordecai included, eventually make their way inside as they get closer and closer to the king.

The author also provides enough information for the reader to form an impression of the palace complex. After Vashti is deposed in chapter 1, the king follows the advice of his servants who suggest that beautiful young virgins from "all the provinces of his kingdom" (2:3) be brought inside to the citadel of Susa. These virgins will in their turn enter the king's bedchamber. And there is also a palace garden, mentioned in 1:5 and 7:7-8, where the seven-day feast is held. Just after Esther reveals that it is Haman who is the "foe and enemy," the king exits in wrath and steps to this palace garden. An "inner court" is mentioned in 4:11, and an "outer court" in 6:4. Haman's house is also alluded to on six separate occasions (5:10; 6:12; 7:9; 8:1, 2, 7), and is located close to the king's residence (7:9). It is here that the gallows are built (7:9), and it is at Haman's house that Mordecai will eventually live.

An important, often mentioned part of the palace complex is the king's gate where Mordecai sits (2:19, 21; 5:13; 6:10).[18] In contrast to Mordecai, Haman is described as sitting only on one occasion—the scene where he and the king sit down for a celebratory drink just after the pogrom edict is dispatched to the provinces (3:15). Haman is a plotter, a contriver, and a man of action who is frequently on his feet. The king's gate may denote the entire palace complex (Fox 1991:38-39), or it may refer

quite literally to a gate of the royal palace (Moore 1971:30).
Outside the king's gate is the "open square" (*rehov ha'ir*) of the
city. This open space, of course, represents an important image
of the literary carnivalesque, and the author often draws our
attention to it. Mordecai leaves the palace complex and enters
the city when he learns that Haman has convinced the king to
issue an edict calling for the destruction of the Jews (4:1). This
open square is also mentioned in 4:6 when Hathach meets Mordecai just outside the king's gate. At 6:11, Mordecai rides
through the open square of the city on a horse (led by none
other than Haman), only to return to the king's gate in the next
verse. The author refers to open space on these and other occasions while concurrently highlighting officialdom's power. As
the plot unfolds, we find quick exits and quick returns to the
center of power, news that originates at the center but which
spreads to the extremities of the concentric circle, and people in
the king's palace who sit next to the king.

Chapters 1–2

Some of the action in this story centers on characters who approach and then depart from the king. As if to call attention to
motion, the author sometimes describes such approaches in
stages and by means of repetition. For example, after Vashti is
deposed, Esther is "taken into the king's palace" (2:8). Just
after we learn that Mordecai is Esther's guardian, the author
reveals that Hegai, who has charge of the women, advances Esther and her maids further to the best place of the harem (2:9).
After a twelve month preparation period, six months with "oil
and myrrh" and six months with "perfumes and cosmetics"
(2:12), the virgins advance even further in the king's palace.
They enter his bedchamber one after another: "In the evening
she went in; then in the morning she came back." The virgins
do not lie with the king again, unless summoned by name
(2:14). Finally, Esther is taken to Ahasuerus's royal bedchamber. The king "loves her more than all the other women" (2:17).
She wins his favor, and is elevated to the rank of queen.

This description of Esther being led to the king in stages is
framed by a description of Mordecai who, in 2:11, walks in

front of the court, and then, at 2:19, sits at the king's gate. Mordecai may reside at the seat of the Susan government (2:5), and is quite possibly a palace official (2:19). He plays a part in the lower ranks of official Persian hierarchy, and this servant of the king may have access to royal quarters (3:2-3). His prominence as one of the king's servants or officials is suggested by the fact that he is close enough to hear of the assassination plot proposed by Bigthan and Teresh, Threshold Guards (2:21). Mordecai's position within the court, whatever it might be, certainly provides him an opportunity to hear of this planned conspiracy, and the narrator describes the information about the assassination plot which moves to the center of the concentric circle of power. Mordecai does not speak to the king directly: his message is conveyed. Mordecai tells Esther, who in turn passes the information on to the king (2:22). Words spoken away from Ahasuerus make their way to his ear, to the very center of power.

Chapter 3-4

Just after chapter 3 opens, Mordecai refuses to bow to Haman, the man whom King Ahasuerus had promoted to a high position above all palace officials. The confrontation, which precipitates the subsequent action in the story, takes place at the king's gate, which the narrator mentions twice (3:2, 3). The servants at the gate bow to Haman, and when they notice that Mordecai does not bow, they ask him why he refuses to honor Haman. The servants eventually tell Haman, but only as late as 3:5 is it reported that Haman sees that Mordecai will not bow down or do obeisance. This delay may suggest that Mordecai's refusal goes unnoticed by Haman at first and that Mordecai was not a member of the highest echelon. He could, therefore, at first escape Haman's attention (Fox 1991:42). Mordecai does reveal his Jewish identity to the servants at the gate (3:4b), and they, after urging him ("they spoke to him day after day" [v. 4]), tell Haman (v. 6). Once again, information has moved near the center of the concentric circle of power, which is now manifest in Haman, whom Ahasuerus has promoted "above all the officials" (3:1). Haman then plots to destroy all the Jews throughout the kingdom. He tells the king about this intractable Mordecai—now the word has reached the very center of power—but twists the details to suit his own purpose:

> There is a certain people scattered and separated among the peoples in all the provinces of your kingdom; their laws are different from those of every other people, and they do not keep the king's laws, so that it is not appropriate for the king to tolerate them (3:8).

As before, someone stands before the king advising him of the implications of an individual who refuses to bow to the powers that be while concurrently suggesting what the king should do. In both instances, one person's action is used as cause for action against a large group of people (i.e., all women and all Jews). Vashti will not be paraded before Ahasuerus's intoxicated guests. Therefore, one suggests, Vashti's action will be made known to the women of Persia and Media and will cause them to "look with contempt on their husbands" (1:17). Now, because Mordecai refuses to bow to Haman, another one suggests that "it is not appropriate for the king to tolerate" (3:8) this people anywhere. Once again, the king complies.

As this news reaches the very center of this concentric circle of power, the narrator passes over the details of Haman's approach to the king: "Then Haman said to King Ahasuerus" (3:8). Queen Esther will later reveal that she and others must receive permission before speaking to the king (4:11); he may not, however, have to grant special permission before Haman can approach the throne. In fact, Haman and Ahasuerus are, we will learn at the end of this scene, drinking buddies. After the edict calling for destruction is written and dispatched, the colleagues who plan genocide sit down for celebratory drinks (3:15).

When Mordecai learns of the forecasted annihilation, he responds by leaving the palace. He laments as he goes "through the city," and then returns "to the entrance of the king's gate" (4:1-2). The author continues the description of spatial coordinates by noting the impact of the edict on those who live at the outer circle, that is, in the provinces: "There was great mourning among the Jews, with fasting and weeping and lamenting, and most of them lay in sackcloth and ashes" (4:3). This description of action moves from the center of the court, out to the provinces, and then back in the direction toward the center of the court. Mordecai approaches the court now wearing sackcloth, and anyone who wears these clothes of mourning is not allowed to pass through the king's gate (4:2). As a result of this communication barrier—the gate now functions as a wall—separating Mordecai on the outside from Esther on the inside, their conversations must be conveyed by a messenger, Hathach, one of the king's eunuchs. Hathach goes out to Mordecai in the open square of the city, which is on the other side of the king's gate (4:6). When Hathach reaches Mordecai, Mordecai conveys the bad news and also gives Hathach a copy of the written decree that calls for the destruction of the Jews. Mordecai encourages Hathach to give this decree to Esther and to tell her to "go to the king" and make entreaty on behalf of her people. His command parallels the previous description in 2:22 where Esther transferred information about the planned assassination from Mordecai to Ahasuerus. David Clines highlights this in-and-out movement: "[the news] must 'track' from the acropolis of Susa (3:15) and the city itself (4:1), to the king's palace (4:13), and its inner court (5:2)."[19]

The city square mentioned in 4:6 is the traditional place for mourning (cf. Amos 5:16; Isa 15:3), and the focus on it highlights the gap that Mordecai and Esther must overcome in order to communicate. Esther first learns that Mordecai is "fasting," "weeping," and "lamenting" in "sackcloth and ashes" from her attending maids and eunuchs (4:3-4). She orders Hathach, one of the eunuchs, to meet with Mordecai and inquire about his psychological condition. The narrator informs us that this meeting takes place in "the open square of the city" in 4:6. Mordecai reveals Haman's plot to Hathach and charges him to ask Esther to make supplication to the king on behalf of her people. After Hathach leaves Mordecai, he returns to Esther and conveys this news from Mordecai. Esther, obviously shocked by Mordecai's plan, gives Hathach yet another message for Mordecai. It is in her second conversation with Hathach that she reveals just how dangerous it is for one to approach the king. She says, "All the king's servants and the people of the king's provinces know that if any man or woman goes to the king inside the inner court without being called, there is but one law—all alike are to be put to death" (4:11a).[20] This "inner court" denotes a place where the king could be seen (cf. 5:1) in contrast to the outer court where he could not (Moore 1971:49; cf. 6:4). As Fox (1991:61) notes, Esther's words suggest a condescending tone: *everybody* knows this. Yet Esther overcomes the universally dreaded law (4:11) by entering and leaving the king's presence unscathed.

This communication via a messenger is highlighted in the next round as "they" tell Mordecai what Esther had said and as Mordecai then tells "them" to respond to Esther once again (4:12-13). To Esther's understandable reluctance, Mordecai responds by suggesting that the reason she has risen and gained access to the inner court is to save her people, that is, to save those whose lives are in danger in that area beyond the official place of power. Then apparently via messenger, Esther responds once again to Mordecai with the instructions that he is to gather the Susan Jews who are outside the king's palace and to hold a three day fast. She reveals that after the fast is complete, she will approach the king, even though this action is against the law (4:16). Esther and Mordecai, on the inside and outside, have overcome the communication barrier.

Chapters 5–7

On the third day after the Mordecai-Hathach-Esther exchanges, Esther dresses in her royal attire and stands in the inner court, opposite the king's hall. The image of her standing before the king is a reminder of her royal status. The king, sitting on his throne, sees Esther. She desires to speak to him, and her wish is granted. When the king sees her, she wins his favor. He holds out the golden scepter to her, an action that allows her to approach him without violating the law. From his words to her, "What is it?" (*mah-lah*), the reader might infer that the king can see her distress. Esther only asks permission to prepare a banquet before the king and Haman, and the king orders Haman brought in so that Esther may have her wish. The scene is particularly provocative because the three people who hold the most power at the court are now, for the first time, in the same room. The king has elevated both Haman and Esther to high positions: Haman to the position of prime minister in 3:1, and Esther to replace Vashti as queen in chapter 2. Both Esther and Haman hold a high office, but it is clear that they are subordinate to the king. Even the queen can approach the king only if he holds out his golden scepter, and Haman for his part had to ask if it pleased the king before a decree was written calling for the destruction of the Jews (3:9).

Instead of telling the king her desire, Esther invites him and Haman to yet another banquet on the following day. Haman is then described as "going out" from the king's presence after he spots Mordecai at the king's gate (5:9). Just as Hathach went out to Mordecai previously (4:6), now Haman goes out as well. Every honor and privilege does Haman no good so long as he sees Mordecai sitting at the king's gate serving among the palace officials. When Haman's wife and friends learn that he is bothered by the mere presence of Mordecai—who again is described as sitting at the king's gate (5:13)—they advise him to have a gallows fifty cubits high built. They also encourage Haman to approach the king and convince him to hang Mordecai on the gallows.

Unaware that the king has suffered from insomnia, had the book of records read to him on the previous night, and been reminded of Mordecai's revelation of the assassination plot against the king, Haman approaches the king the next morning. The entire scene is narrated with description and dialogue often suggesting spatial coordinates. This latest approach to the center of power is conveyed by the king who asks, "Who is in the court?" (6:4). The narrator then provides a comment, as if to make the spatial reference clear: "Now Haman had just entered the outer court of the king's palace to speak to the king about having Mordecai hanged" (6:4b). The servants will underscore this reference once again in the next verse in their speech to the king: "Haman is there, standing in the court." Like Esther before (5:1), Haman now stands in the inner court waiting for an audience with the king. After Haman enters, the king asks what should be done for the person whom the king wishes to honor. Haman, thinking of himself, advises the king to let this man wear the royal robes, to ride on the king's own horse, and to be escorted "through the open square of the city" proclaiming the news, "thus shall it be done for the man whom the king wishes to honor" (6:9). The king instructs Haman to "do so to the Jew Mordecai who sits at the king's gate" (6:10), and the narrator, echoing Haman, tells us that this news spreads "through the open square of the city" (6:11). Immediately after this parade, the two men, Mordecai and Haman, return, so to speak, toward the center of official power. Mordecai goes to the king's gate and Haman to his own house, mourning with his head covered (6:12). Shortly thereafter, Haman is hurried off by the king's eunuchs and gets even closer to the king at the second banquet which Esther has prepared.

The critical scene in chapter 7 features three powerful characters once again: the king, Haman, who is the enemy of the Jews, and Esther, who now has the opportunity of standing beside the king and speaking to him on behalf of her people. It is in this scene that she finally reveals that Haman is the one who has sold the queen and her people to be destroyed, killed, and annihilated. The motif of quick exit and quick return reappears as the king rises from the feast in wrath and exits to the palace garden (v. 7), only to return (v. 8) to find Haman on the couch, just beside Esther. Haman is pleading for his life, but, from Ahasuerus's eyes, it looks more like an attack on the queen: "Will he even assault the queen in my presence, in my own house?" (v. 8). One of the eunuchs, Harbona, calls to the king's attention the pole in Haman's courtyard prepared for the impalement of Mordecai (v. 9). At this prompting—once again!—the king orders Haman to be hanged on the gallows that Haman had prepared for Mordecai.

Chapters 8–10

Just after Haman is hanged on the gallows, King Ahasuerus gives Haman's house to Queen Esther. Mordecai then "comes before the king." Now that the king knows that Mordecai and Esther are relatives, Mordecai is apparently in no danger as he approaches the king. Yet one central element of the story remains to be resolved. Haman's edict still stands. In fact, it cannot be revoked (8:8)! Esther, in close proximity to the king, speaks once again on behalf of her people, the folk who live outside this concentric circle of power. The narrator describes these spatial coordinates in some detail: she falls at his feet; he holds out the golden scepter; she rises and stands before the king (8:3-5). Esther asks permission for an order to be written to revoke the pogrom edict that Haman had devised. An edict is written, this time according to Mordecai's command, and, once again, official word from the inner circle goes out all the way from India to Ethiopia (8:9). The edict, universal in scope, does not revoke the previous one which called for the destruction of the Jews; it merely allows Jews to defend themselves (8:11). It is written for everyone in the "one hundred twenty-seven provinces, to every province in its own script and to every people in its own language, and also to the Jews in their script and their language" (8:9). After the decree is issued in Susa, the narrator describes Mordecai going out from the presence of the king. The news is spread by means of fast steeds bred from the royal herd, and as it goes out there is "gladness, joy, and honor" for the Jews of Susa first of all, and then eventually in all the provinces in the outlying cities. This good news spreads to the outer limits of the concentric circles, and "many of the peoples of the country professed to be Jews, because the fear of the Jews had fallen upon them" (8:17).

This survey of the plot reveals that the author uses images of the public square and the streets adjoining to contrast life that is far removed from the crown with life in the palace, the place of official order, power, and ideology. While we do not quite find the "extraordinary spatial and temporal expanses that leap at us from the pages of Rabelais' novel," (Bakhtin 1981: 167), we do see that the author describes movement to and from the center of power as the plot unfolds.

4

PERIPETY

Abuse with uncrowning, as truth about the old authority,
about the dying world, is an organic part of Rabelais' system
of images.
—Mikhail Bakhtin, *Rabelais and His World*

THE CARNIVALESQUE AND PERIPETY

Since Bakhtin is concerned with texts as social phenomena, it
is not surprising to find him observing that the state of society
is sometimes one where social classes and hierarchies exist.
Such distinctions and hierarchies are often rigid and oppressive
in nature, and in such an environment one discovers what is
and what is not permitted. Carnival celebrates the opposite of
such rigid forms. If the state symbol is a uniform that turns its
wearer into an unambiguous sign of rank, then carnival's symbol is the mask that veils identity and thus makes transformation
possible. The ambivalence of language in the public square led
Bakhtin to the conclusion that carnival images are formed in
terms of antitheses: birth and death, youth and old age, top and
bottom, praise and abuse, sacred and profane, sublime and infamous, sacred texts and carnival sacrileges.

At this point, we may once again consider the relationship
between literature and folk culture. Bakhtin claims that a few
literary texts mirror carnivalesque actions. Rabelais's work in
particular reflects folk culture's acts, and his language system
reconstructs the linguistic forms of carnival language. Bakhtin
calls the process of transposition from carnival language with its
specific worldview and categories into the language of literature
the "carnivalization of literature." With this transposition, one
witnesses an overturning of a world (replete with hierarchical

80

order) and a turnabout in values, thoughts, and actions in the texts themselves.

To illustrate his point on a world turned upside down, Bakhtin makes the following observation in his book on Rabelais:

> Carnival celebrates the destruction of the old and the birth of the new world—the new year, the new spring, the new kingdom. The old world that has been destroyed is offered together with the new world and is represented with it as the dying part of the dual body. This is why in carnivalesque images there is so much turnabout, so many opposite faces and intentionally upset proportions (1984b:410).

From this vantage point Bakhtin studies the various forms of inversion, reversals, or displacements in the hierarchical top to bottom in carnival. He pays particular attention to the ritual of changing clothes, that is, to the renewal of clothes and their social image (a topic which is explored in the following sections). For this reason, one finds in carnival an abundance of deliberately violated proportions and numerous images of the inside-out. If turnabout is a central feature of the literary carnivalesque, it is not surprising to find that the plot of Esther unfolds by a series of peripeties—sudden and unexpected reversals of circumstance or situation whereby intended actions produce the opposite results. Commentators have often noted the many reversals in the book,[1] but have, as far as I can tell, overlooked their role as key components of the carnivalesque itself.

ESTHER AND PERIPETY

Instead of a linear sequence of events, the Esther plot unfolds by reversals—not changes or breakdowns, but specific 180 degree turns. The force of evil is not merely overcome; it turns back on itself. Haman unwittingly volunteers the method by which his archenemy, Mordecai, is honored by the king (6: 6-11). The narrator turns Haman's thoughts, "Whom would the king wish to honor more than me?," back on Haman. After suggesting that the person chosen be allowed to don the king's royal robes and royal crown and ride the king's royal horse,

Haman hears the king say, "Quickly, take the robes and the horse, as you have said, and do so to"—Haman expects to hear his own name, but instead hears his enemy's—"the Jew Mordecai" (6:10). Haman's best laid plans also produce the opposite of what's hoped for on another occasion: He is hanged from the gallows he had built for Mordecai. The narrator reports that when Esther came before the king, "he gave orders in writing that the wicked plot that [Haman] had devised against the Jews should come upon his own head, and that he and his sons should be hanged on the gallows" (9:25).[2] Justice through peripety emerges as an important theme in this story where power and loyalties are reversed.

Fear of women ruling over men is expressed early in the story. Vashti's refusal to appear at the king's command will cause "all women" throughout the kingdom, Memucan relates, "to look with contempt on their husbands" (1:17). In addition, "the noble ladies of Persia and Media who have heard of the queen's behavior will rebel against the king's officials, and there will be no end of contempt and wrath!" (1:18). Memucan advises that Vashti should never come before the king and that her royal position be given to someone else. This punishment, Memucan thinks, will cause "all women [to] give honor to their husbands" (1:20). But this is the narrative world of turnabout: halfway through the story Haman will seek the advice of his wife (5:10-14); Mordecai will also turn to Esther for help (chap. 3), and she will plot against Haman during the course of two separate banquets (chaps. 5 and 7). The influence and power that Esther wields become increasingly apparent as the story unfolds. For example, she manages and manipulates the men: Haman, Ahasuerus, even Mordecai. She takes the initiative by commanding Mordecai to act on her behalf: "Go, gather all the Jews to be found in Susa, and hold a fast on my behalf, and neither eat nor drink for three days, night or day" (4:16). Mordecai had commanded Esther just after this story opened, but now it is Esther who commands Mordecai: go, gather, fast, don't eat, and don't drink. The narrator reveals the extent of her rise to power and influence at the conclusion of the scene: Mordecai "did everything as Esther had ordered him" (4:17).

Such obedience reverses our expectations of the roles men and women will assume as forecasted in the opening chapter (cf. 1:10-11, 15-20, and esp. 1:22b). With Mordecai in the background, Esther executes the plan. *She*, following the prompting of Mordecai, creates the conditions whereby Haman is unmasked with her clever, self-effacing words, "If we had been sold merely as slaves, men and women, I would have held my peace." *She* draws the central question out of the king, "Who is he, and where is he, who has presumed to do this?" Now the time is right, Esther knows, for her to say, "A foe and enemy, this wicked Haman!" (7:4-6). With the king angry, Esther is in good position to respond: Who is he, you ask. A foe and an enemy, that's who, this wicked Haman. She breaks her silence on this matter because of her concern for her people and her loyalty to the crown by implying that the Jews' enemy, Haman, is one who deceives the king and threatens his rule: "But no enemy can compensate for this damage to the king" (7:4). Esther's high position is also suggested by her part in Mordecai's promotion: "Mordecai came before the king, for Esther had revealed how he was related to her" (8:1). She, not Ahasuerus, sets Mordecai over Haman's house.

Esther's protracted rise is only one example of reversals in this story (cf. 1:22b). The sequence of paired oppositions is sometimes found within a brief narrative space, and, by placing oppositions in close proximity, the phenomenon of peripety is accentuated. Just after the first banquet that Esther prepares for Haman and Ahasuerus, Haman exits the palace "happy and in good spirits" (5:9a). He spots Mordecai at the king's gate, observes that Mordecai neither rises nor trembles before him, and, from the narrator's description once again of the inner life, we discover that Haman is now, suddenly, "infuriated with Mordecai" (5:9b). We observe this similar sea change in proud Haman whose swelling ego is quickly deflated in the next chapter when he encourages the king to dress the man in royal garments whom the king wishes to honor, only to discover that the king has Mordecai in mind (6:6-10).

On another occasion Haman turns around within a brief narrative space, just after the king's sleepless night episode of chapter 6. Haman receives counsel in the collective voice of his wife and friends ("his wife Zeresh and all his friends said to him . . .") who advise him to build a gallows fifty cubits high, to tell the king in the morning to have Mordecai hanged on it, and then to approach the king at the banquet "in good spirits" (5:14). At the end of chapter 6, Haman returns home from the banquet, that is, on the spatial plane he makes an about face, and his good spirits have been altered. Now he is "mourning" and his head is covered. Haman again receives collective advice ("his advisers and his wife Zeresh said to him . . ."), and their words reinforce the turn of affairs: "If Mordecai, before whom *your downfall* has begun, is of the Jewish people, you will not prevail against him, *but will surely fall before him*" (6:13; emphasis added). These reversals and oppositions are in this instance reinforced by the narrator who parallels words and images:

his wife Zeresh and all his friends said to him /
his advisers and his wife Zeresh said to him.
Haman builds gallows to be used on Mordecai /
Haman's gallows are used on Haman.

At other times, the reversals are prolonged. The pervasive sense of tragedy conveyed in the opening chapters is transformed, but only by the book's end, into a gay, happy, and even comic celebration. When the once powerless Jews attain power at the story's end, their fasts become joyous celebratory feasts, and the final feasting and celebration is a reversal of the fasting and weeping that occurred just after Haman's genocide-edict was published earlier in the story. The narrator highlights this major reversal at the end: "on *the very day* when the enemies of the Jews hoped to gain power over them, but which had been changed to a day when the Jews would gain power over their foes" (9:1; emphasis added). The reversal happens on the appointed day of destruction as Jews gain power when their enemies had hoped to gain power, and the fourfold depiction of joy with abstract terms (light, gladness, joy, and honor) in 8:16 obviously reverses the four nouns that signalled gloom in 4:3, mourning, fasting, weeping, and lamenting (Clines 1984:97).

Mordecai also describes these sudden, unexpected turn of events in the letter that he writes and sends to Jews in all provinces. He encourages them to make the fourteenth and fifteenth day of Adar an annual day of celebration because it was on these days that "the Jews gained relief from their enemies, and [on this month that events] had been turned for them from sorrow into gladness and from mourning into a holiday" (9:22).

The reversal that occupies the most narrative space in this story is found in the parallel passages of 3:9-4:3 and 8:2-17. These two passages are listed in the table on pp. 86 and 87, and corresponding elements of the plot are noted (1, 1', 2, 2', and so forth) in the table and accompanying narrative summary.[3] Both passages deal with the issue of authority and the focus is on decree writing, counter decree writing, and decree dispatching. The verbatim parallels, marked with italicized words in the second series, accentuate the similarity of the two scenes. Reversals, on the other hand, are suggested by the non-italicized words in the second series, and the uniqueness of item "X" in the second series highlights the fact that the change of affairs does not merely involve Haman and Mordecai. Esther is introduced as a pivotal player in this transfer of power.[4]

Important turnabouts are found at a number of places in the second narrative block. In both scenes the king takes off his signet ring and gives it to someone else—in the first episode to Haman (2), and in the second to Mordecai (2'). Mordecai receives this symbol of power that Haman had previously held, and to accentuate Haman's decline, the narrator adds the explanatory words in the second series of this reversal to highlight the main point: the king takes the ring *from Haman* and then gives it to Mordecai.

In the second round, when Esther begins her petition with the king by saying, "If it pleases the king" (1'), she duplicates the words that Haman spoke previously (1). She, like Haman, asks for a written order. His purpose in asking for the decree was to call for the destruction of the Jews; her purpose in asking for a decree now is to undo the previous decree. The reversal is accomplished by means of duplicated speech: "If it

Plot Components of 3:9–4:3

1   "If it pleases the king, let a decree be written for their destruction."

2   So the king took off his signet ring from his hand and gave it to Haman son of Hammedatha the Agagite, the enemy of the Jews.

3   And the king said to Haman, "The money is given to you, and the people as well, to do with them as it seems good to you."

4   Then the king's secretaries were summoned on the thirteenth day of the first month, and an edict was written, according to all that Haman commanded, to the king's satraps and to the governors over all the provinces and to the officials of all the peoples, to every province in its own script and to every people in its own language; it was written in the name of King Ahasuerus and sealed with the king's ring.

5   Letters were sent by couriers to all the king's provinces, giving orders to destroy, to kill, and to annihilate all Jews, young and old, children and women, on a single day, the thirteenth day of the twelfth month, which is the month of Adar, and to plunder their goods.

6   A copy of the document was to be issued as a decree in every province and to be made known to all the people to be ready for that day.

7   So the couriers hurried out, urged by the king's command, and the decree was issued in the citadel of Susa.

8   The king and Haman sat down to drink; but the city of Susa was thrown into confusion.

9   When Mordecai learned all that had been done, Mordecai tore his clothes and put on sackcloth and ashes, and he went out into the city, wailing with a loud and bitter cry. . . .

10 In every province, wherever the king's command and his decree came, there was great mourning among the Jews, with fasting and weeping and lamenting, and many of them lay in sackcloth and ashes.

Plot Components of 8:2-17

2' *So the king took off his signet ring,* which he had taken from Haman, *and gave it to* Mordecai.

X   So Esther set Mordecai over the house of Haman. . . .

1' *"If it pleases the king, . . . let a decree be written* to revoke the letters devised by Haman son of Hammedatha the Agagite, which he wrote giving orders to destroy the Jews who are in all the provinces of the king. . . ."

3' And *King* Ahasuerus *said to* Queen Esther and to the Jew Mordecai, "See, I have *given* Esther the house of Haman, and they have hanged him on the gallows, because he plotted to lay hands on the Jews. You may write *as it seems good to you* with regard to the Jews, in the name of the king, and seal it with the king's ring; for an edict written in the name of the king and sealed with the king's ring cannot be revoked."

4' *Then the king's secretaries were summoned* at that time, in the third month, which is the month of Sivan, on the twenty-third day; *and an edict was written, according to all that* Mordecai *commanded,* to the Jews and *to the satraps and to the governors and the officials* of the provinces from India to Ethiopia, one hundred twenty-seven provinces, *to every province in its own script and to every people in its own language,* and also to the Jews in their script and their language. He wrote letters *in the name of King Ahasuerus, sealed* them *with the king's ring,* and *sent them by* mounted *couriers* riding on fast steeds bred from the royal herd.

5' By these letters the king allowed the Jews who were in every city to assemble and defend their lives, *to destroy, to kill, and to annihilate* any armed force of any people or province that might attach them, with their *children and women,* and *to plunder their goods on a single day* throughout all the provinces of King Ahasuerus, on *the thirteenth day of the twelfth month, which is the month of Adar.*

6' *A copy of the document was to be issued as a decree in every province and to be made known to all the people,* and the Jews were *to be ready for that day* to take revenge on their enemies.

7' *So the couriers,* mounted on their swift royal steeds, *hurried out, urged by the king's command, and the decree was issued in the citadel of Susa.*

9' Then *Mordecai went out* away from the presence of the king, wearing royal robes of blue and white, with a great golden crown and a mantle of fine linen and purple, while the city of Susa shouted and rejoiced. . . .

10' *In every province* and in every city, *wherever the king's command and his decree came, there was* gladness and joy *among the Jews,* a festival and a holiday.

pleases the king, let a decree be written." The narrator portrays Esther, who was not present during the first dialogue event, invoking the very words that Haman spoke previously. She reveals her strategy just after duplicating Haman's words by adding that the purpose of this counter-decree is "to revoke the letters devised by Haman, son of Hammedatha the Agagite, which he wrote." The edict was originally signed and sealed in the *king's name*, but Esther does not dare mention that now. What she hopes to convey with her verbal dexterity is Haman's responsibility, and, by not mentioning Ahasuerus's role, she may be able to convince the king that an individual's scheme can be overwritten more easily than can a complex, official administrative order. From the reader's vantage point, the (unnecessary) mention of "the Agagite" might conjure old images of Israelite animosity toward the Amalekites at the time of Balaam's oracles (Num 24:7, 20) or King Agag in his confrontation with Saul (1 Sam 15). But for the speaker and addressee, these multiple references to Haman shift attention away from the king's complicity.

The idea of giving "as it seems good to you" is duplicated in the second series (3'). At first, Ahasuerus gives money to Haman and the people to do with as they please (3).[5] In the second round, the king gives Esther the house that belonged to Haman, and Esther sets Mordecai over Haman's house. The descriptions of the edict dispatch and the counter-edict are also similar (4 and 4'). They contain numerous verbal parallels: secretaries are summoned; an edict is written following someone's command; it is sent to the satraps, governors, and officials; it goes to every province in languages understood by all the people; and it is written in the name of the king and sealed with his ring. But in the second sequence the edict is written according to all that Mordecai commands. In addition, the author adds the phrase in 4', "and also to the Jews in their script and their language," a reminder that the Jewish people are now recognized as a national and political force. The language of the Jews gains official status. Indeed, unofficial culture has overcome what appeared to be insurmountable obstacles in this carnivalesque world.

In both instances, the letters contain instructions "to destroy, to kill, and to annihilate . . . children and women . . . on a single day . . . the thirteenth day of the twelfth month, which is the month of Adar" (5 and 5'). But with this duplication, the potential murderers and victims are crisscrossed. X : Y becomes Y : X. Accordingly, "the people" are to be ready for that day in the first round, but in the second sequence it is "the Jews" who are to be ready for that day (6 and 6'). The Jews reverse the projected outcome by taking "revenge on their enemies" (6'). In the parallel passages, 9 and 9', Mordecai "goes out" just after the decrees are issued in the citadel of Susa, and the narrator's description of his clothes underscores the change in political wind. At first, he tears them after learning the news of the decree (9), but after the second decree is issued, he dons the royal blue and white robes and accessories such as the golden crown, and mantle of fine linen and purple (9'). Mordecai now wears garments that would have signified a high royal position in the ancient Near East.[6] Finally, the narrator describes the turn of affairs for the Jewish people who first of all "mourn," "fast," "weep," and "lament" (10), but then rejoice in "gladness" and "joy" on the "festival" and "holiday" (10').

The focus in this section has been on peripety, one of the distinguishing characteristics of the carnivalesque whereby plot actions turn 180 degrees. The preponderance of such reversals supports the view that the Esther (M) story belongs to the serio-comical (*spoudogeloios* or "serious-smiling") genre, and the mention of Mordecai's garments serves as a transition in our discussion. We will now look more closely at things worn (clothes, crowns, and masks for example) as we ask questions about their place in the literary carnivalesque.

THE CARNIVALESQUE: BODY AND CLOTHES

In *Rabelais and His World*, Mikhail Bakhtin offers an exhaustive study of what he calls the "popular-festive forms" (eating, drinking, cursing, and abusing) and "the grotesque images of the body" (sex, defecation, birth, and death). To him, the unabashed display of the body and bodily functions during carnival time does not suggest anything negative; rather, "with all its images, indecencies, and curses, [carnival] affirms the people's immortal, indestructible character" (1984b:256). Bakhtin arrives at this positive view of carnival dialectically by focusing on what the human body represented in earlier times. During the Middle Ages and Renaissance, conceptions of the world were transferred to the body itself. The body became "the relative center of the cosmos" (1984b:363), which the Renaissance philosophers discussed in terms of two characteristic tendencies: "First is the tendency to find in man [and woman] the entire universe with all its elements and forces, with its higher and lower stratum; second is the tendency to think of the human body as drawing together the most remote phenomena and forces of the cosmos" (1984b:365).[7] In this discussion, Bakhtin's prime concern is the return of the body in the Renaissance, whereby the revaluation of the body's role in the cosmos is decisive:

> All things in the universe, from heavenly bodies to elements, had left their former place in their hierarchy and moved to the single horizontal plane of the world of becoming, where they began to seek a new place and to achieve new formations. The center around which these perturbations took place was precisely the human body, uniting all the varied patterns of the universe (1984b:365).

Here one finds a reformulation of the Renaissance philosophical concept in which a human being exists as something bound within a universal sympathy, with a corresponding relation between micro- and macrocosm.

In their biography of Mikhail Bakhtin, Katerina Clark and Michael Holquist provide an account of his long bout with osteomyelitis and the amputation of his right leg (1984:27). This great celebrator of the body and bodily processes was, all his adult life, a sick man, physically very circumscribed. Yet he is able to discern in the festival laughter of the folk in the marketplace or open square a preoccupation with the body and with bodily functions. During carnival time, the folk overcome oppression by celebrating the body. They laugh to degrade all official or abstract conceptions about earthiness or body-concentration. The primary element in carnival, the "free-intermingling of bodies," is their response to official culture which regards such bodily functions as unseemly, which would stop the joyous celebration of earth, body, and life. Bakhtin emphasizes again and again that this celebration is always opposed to that put forward by official culture which seeks to reduce earth, body, and life to a flat plane.

It is Rabelais in particular who joins forces with the medieval and Renaissance laughter tradition. He uses festival-marketplace bodily signs and images to degrade and uncrown all abstract notions of propriety. For example, in the famous opening scene in Book I of *Gargantua and Pantagruel*, we discover that Gargantua's mother overeats on tripe which in turn causes complications at the time of delivery. The child enters a "hollow vein" and ascends "to a point above her shoulders [where] the vein divides into two." From there, the child accordingly "works his way in a sinistral direction, to issue, finally, through the left ear" (Rabelais 1936:22-23). While discussing this episode, Bakhtin concludes that "the merry, abundant and victorious bodily element opposes the serious medieval world of fear and oppression with all its intimidating and intimidated ideology" (1984b:226). From such a passage in Rabelais, and from other writers of the carnivalesque, we discover that carnival celebrates the body and earth while reducing absolute and abstract thinking.

The dismembered body and anatomization also play a considerable part in the literary carnivalesque:

> The scene of the scandal and decrowning of the prince—the carnival king, or more accurately the carnival bridegroom—is consistently portrayed as a *tearing to pieces*, as a typical carnivalistic 'sacrificial' dismemberment into parts. . . . Carnivalization allows [authors of the carnivalesque] to glimpse and bring to life aspects in the character and behavior of people which in the normal course of life could not have revealed themselves (1984a:161-63; original emphasis).

Turning to the book of Esther, one may be struck by high ranking members of official culture who participate in banquets, especially in chapters 1 and 2. In contrast to later carnivalesque forms, official culture does celebrate here. The king, officials, ministers, nobles, and governors of the provinces all participate in carnival-like banquets. For her part, Vashti also sponsors a banquet, confined in narrative space to only one verse.[8] Though she sponsors a banquet, she is herself subject to the whims of her husband and is certainly not a full member of official culture. When she refuses to display herself before bibulous men, her husband, with all his official power, summons the sages who know the laws. Memucan advises that an unalterable royal order be written among the laws that would forever ban her from the king's presence (1:19).

ESTHER: BODY AND CLOTHES

We certainly do not find in the story of Esther the grotesque imagery of the body, the animal forms, and the inanimate objects that the body acquires in late carnival. But images of the body are sometimes in the background or foreground in the Esther narrative: Ahasuerus hopes to parade his wife before all the partygoers so that they may admire her beauty (1:11),[9] and the virgins undergo a twelve-month cosmetic treatment before the king summons them by name to his bed (2:12-14). Dismemberment, a major element in full-blown carnivalesque plots, also occasionally figures in the Esther narrative as two overarching questions emerge from the plot: Will the Jews be destroyed, killed, and annihilated (3:13)? And will Mordecai be hanged as Haman intends (5:14)? Of course, as the audience moves from these early forecasts to enactment scenes, the would-be body victimizers become the actual victims (7:10, 8:11; 9:1-10). Even Haman's ten sons are hanged from the gallows (9:13-14). While dismemberment does not play as significant a role in the story as it does in later carnivalesque writings, one does discover that the ancient author gives considerable attention to appearance, especially to clothes and other items that characters wear. The change of clothing motif is important because it highlights role reversals, and it is not by accident that a tradition of wearing costumes and masks develops as part of the Purim celebration. The Esther scroll contains a number of references to clothes, jewelry, and role reversals. Let us consider a few scenes.

A Cosmetic Treatment

When the confusion of the opening scene subsides, Ahasuerus "remembers Vashti and what she had done and what had been decreed against her" (2:1). Perhaps the king remembers her beauty—a quality that he obviously admires in women—for his servants are quick to suggest a comprehensive plan whereby beautiful virgins will be brought before him: commissioners from "all" the provinces are to gather "all" the beautiful young virgins throughout the kingdom and bring them to the citadel of Susa. She who "pleases the king," they suggest, should replace Vashti as queen (2:2-4). The plan apparently appeals to the king: he wastes no time in implementing it (2:4). This literary motif of the beautiful maiden summoned to the king's bed is found both within and outside the Bible. King Shekriya summoned a new woman each night in the *Arabian Nights*, and a beautiful bed-partner is found for the ailing King David in 1 Kgs 1:1-4 (Fox 1991:28; Bardtke 1963:295-96). While the motif is not new, the combined images of Esther's beauty, the clothes she wears, and the cosmetic treatments she receives give the scene a distinct carnivalesque aura.

Just after Esther is brought to the harem in the citadel of Susa, she is given a special, if not gaudy, treatment. She wins the favor of Hegai, the king's chief eunuch in charge of the women, who quickly provides her with cosmetic treatments, food, and seven maids from the king's palace. He also advances Esther and the maids who wait on her to the best place in the harem (2:9). Before any of the virgins enter the king's bedchamber, they must receive the beauty treatment which lasts no less than twelve months—a six-month massage with oil and myrrh and a six-month treatment with balsam and other cosmetics (2:12; cf. Moore 1971:23). This beauty treatment ritual and the giving of food is an act of *hesed* or "goodwill," which here conveys the actions of a superior to an inferior, which Esther, at this stage of the story, obviously is (Fox 1991:31).

Notice that the will of the women, whatever it was, is passed over altogether by the narrator, suggesting—and perhaps this is what is most oppressive of all—that the perspective of the virgins who are summoned is of no consequence. In fact, they are never described as being "forced" into the king's quarters. It is assumed in this carnivalesque narrative world that their bodies belong to someone else.[10] In the midst of this description of Esther's appearance, we should not lose sight of the fact that one purpose, especially at 2:5-7, is to introduce Esther in *relationship* to her cousin Mordecai.

The kind of lavish royal treatment that Esther receives in this passage is entirely consistent with the exaggerated, carnivalesque imagery of the opening banquet scenes. The excess is accentuated in chapter 2 by Esther's natural beauty and passivity. While describing Mordecai, the narrator informs us that he is cousin and guardian of Esther who is "fair and beautiful" (v. 7). When Esther's turn comes to enter the king's bedchamber, the narrator draws attention once again to her appearance: "Esther was admired by all who saw her" (v. 15). She does not reveal any eagerness to be elevated as queen. She is first of all "gathered" in the citadel of Susa (v. 8); then "provided" cosmetic treatments, food, and maids (v. 9); "advanced" to the best place in the harem (v. 9); "taken" to the king's bedroom (v. 16); and then finally "made" queen (v. 17). Apparently, some virgins ask for whatever they desire to take with them to the king's palace (v. 13), and Carey Moore concludes, though without textual support, that some took advantage of the opportunity to gratify their personal desires by asking for jewelry and clothes (1971: 24). But Esther asks only for Hegai's advice. She trusts him to tell her what she might put on to make herself appealing to the king.

The Queen's New Clothes

In an obvious reversal from Vashti's behavior in the opening scene, Esther is passive and cooperative in chapter 2. We will learn that she is also intelligent and courageous. She will wait for the right moment to speak on behalf of her people. The passive Esther of the opening chapters will one day take matters into her own hands, and this important reversal is narrated with attention on, once again, what Esther is wearing. Several important events transpire from the time the narrator mentions Esther's appearance in chapter 2 to the beginning of chapter 5, where the narrator describes Esther's clothes: Esther is made queen (2:17); after being informed by Mordecai, she tells her husband of a plot to assassinate the king (2:22); Haman becomes prime minister (3:1); Mordecai refuses to bow to him (3:2, 5); an edict is issued calling for the destruction of the Jews (3:12-15); and Mordecai encourages Esther not to keep silent at such a time as this (4:14). Finally Esther takes the initiative and approaches the king, "though it is against the law" (4:16). She "puts on her royal robes" (5:1) and stands in full view of the king. Esther is this time arrayed in full royal dress (*malkut*). Unlike the scene in chapter 2, Esther is not just wearing the kind of attractive clothes and costly jewelry that Hegai recommended (v. 15). She has now put on clothes that match her royal stature. The use of the word *malekut* is important because without a qualifier the narrator hints at a comparison between her royal status and Ahasuerus's. Esther is not merely dressing up as queen, but is "putting on royally" (Fox 1991:67-68). The word is also important from a contextual standpoint. Mordecai had used it earlier in 4:14: "Perhaps you have come to royalty (*malkut*) for such a time as this." And in 5:1 the root *mlk* is used to denote the position of Ahasuerus: "the king's palace" (*bet hammelek*) is mentioned twice, and the "royal throne" (*kisse' malkut*) and "royal palace" (*bet hammalkut*) each occur once (Berg 1979:87 n. 44). Therefore, the reference to Esther's royal clothes in chapter 5 subtly conveys her rise to power and influence at this stage of the story. Indeed, as Fox observes, this image reveals not only her "station but a personal quality" (1991:67-68; cf. Berg 1979:70, 87 n. 44). Yet she is obviously a subordinate. Even the queen in her "royal robes" is violating the law when she approaches the king unbidden.

The two clothes scenes (chaps. 2 and 5) are linked by the attention given to Esther's garments and by the king's perception of them. In 2:4, it is the one who appears "good in the king's eyes" that will be chosen queen. In 5:2, Esther "finds favor in his sight"—despite the three-day-neither-food-nor-drink fast that she undertook (4:16). But the king and queen are not the only ones in this story who wear royal clothes.

If royal robes are the symbol of power and exuberance,

sackcloth is certainly their opposite. After Mordecai learns of Haman's plan to annihilate the Jews, a plan that has been set in motion by the royal secretarial apparatus (3:12-15), he tears his clothes, puts on sackcloth and ashes, and cries out bitterly (4:1). Such combined actions were conventional religious acts, but here they may serve exclusively to highlight the expression of grief (cf. Gen 37:29; 2 Kgs 18:37; Job 7:5). Prayer sometimes accompanied fasting (Jer 14:11-12; Ezra 8:21, 23; Neh 9:1; Jonah 3:7-8), and thus the omission of it and God's name here in Esther is certainly consistent with what we have already observed: the author avoids dwelling on explicit religious ideas and vocabulary. The scene in Esther, like so many, has a decidedly carnivalesque cast.

Mordecai goes through the city wailing (4:1), until he finally approaches the entrance of the king's gate (4:2). He excludes himself from the court by dressing in sackcloth, for no one may enter the king's gate dressed like this. The narrator's description of Mordecai's actions with spatial references is cleverly ambiguous. What motivates Mordecai to go up to the king's gate dressed in sackcloth? Is there a provocative action behind his grieving? Is he now obeying a custom, or calling attention to how he might disobey it? Perhaps his going up to the king's gate dressed in mourning garb is meant to suggest that he no longer fears any punishment for acts of disobedience. Even though the Hebrew indicates that he goes "up to" (*'ad liphne*), rather than what is forbidden, "into" (*'el*), the king's gate, Mordecai may be threatening once again to disregard Persian law and custom. As Danna Nolan Fewell has suggested, when Esther responds by sending garments to clothe Mordecai "so that he might take off his sackcloth" (4:4), she may be hoping to keep him from aggravating an already grievous situation (Fox 1991:58 n. 34). At least three not entirely incompatible interpretations suggest themselves. First, Mordecai may be lamenting his own misery. After all, it is his refusal to bow to Haman that precipitates Haman's response, which in turn jeopardizes Mordecai's life. Second, he may be mourning the fate of his people. The orders are to kill "*all* Jews, young and old, women and children" (3:13). Third, he might also wish to prompt Esther into

96

action. His actions certainly produce consequences on both sides of the king's gate. Outside, the Jews in all provinces begin fasting, weeping, and lamenting, and many dress in sackcloth and cover themselves with ashes. Esther, inside the palace, becomes deeply distressed at Mordecai's actions, and the narrator provides a description of her response that, once again, involves clothes: "she sends garments to clothe Mordecai, so that he might take off his sackcloth; but he would not accept them" (4:4).

The narrator may be hinting in these descriptions of outward appearance that Mordecai is engaging in a tactical move.[11] Indeed, Mordecai will soon encourage Esther to take a chance with her own life on behalf of the Jewish people. By "sending" garments to clothe Mordecai, the narrator anticipates other actions. Mordecai and Esther will "send" messages via Hathach, and Hathach will eventually ask Esther to make supplication for the Jewish people. "Sending" messengers allows for literary connections and complications, and is a favorite device among Hebrew biblical authors. One famous example is 2 Samuel 11. With respect to this passage from Esther, David Clines makes the following astute observation about "clothes" and "sending":

> We should add to this mastery of structural function some details of narrative subtlety. We can concentrate first on the objects of 'sending'. Against the colourfully painted backdrop of the edict's being 'sent' by couriers throughout the empire (3.13), in 4.8 we find Mordecai sending into the palace not just the news of the decree but a written copy of the edict. It is a physical counterpart of the clothes that Esther has sent out in the previous communication scene (v. 4), but unlike the clothes, the edict is a token that cannot be refused. This is because with clothes Mordecai has a choice, but with the edict there is no choice. There is no counter-edict (though there is a 'counter' set of clothes)—at least there is no counter-edict yet. When there is, Mordecai will wear palace clothes, royal robes of blue and white (8.15), and, proleptically, even before there is, but as soon as the balance has begun to tip in the Jews' favour, Mordecai will have the use of royal robes temporarily, for a day. Now, in ch. 4, the edict is the clothing that Esther must 'wear' (1984:34-35).

Haman Desires the King's Clothes

Perhaps the scene that conveys the most obvious and direct reversal of clothes imagery is found at 6:8-11. According to one commentator, it is in this scene that "the plot takes its sharpest turn" (Fox 1991:162). In conversation with the king, Haman learns that Ahasuerus wishes to honor someone. Haman assumes that the person in question is none other than himself, so he describes a ceremony in which the honoree will be given the king's clothes, the king's horse, even a parade that will be led by one of the king's most noble officials. He hopes the ceremony will take place publicly—through the open square of the city with the king's official shouting, "Thus shall it be done for the man whom the king wishes to honor" (6:9). Haman suggests this parade to the king and calls for nothing less than a display of the highest honors (a royal robe, horse, and crown) and an ostentatious show that is reminiscent of the flaunting described in chapter 1. Notice in 6:8 that Haman's request is not merely for those things that the king owns, but for robes *that the king has worn* and a horse *that the king has ridden*. There can be little doubt that anyone donning the king's robe and riding the king's horse stands in great favor, and, by dressing up like this, Haman hopes to put on the king's aura. Indeed, Haman would warm to the idea of being king, but the narrator informs us that Ahasuerus announces that the honoree is none other than the "Jew Mordecai" (6:10). In this turnabout, Haman, the would-be-honoree, is commanded to execute this plan by robing Mordecai and then leading him through the streets, shouting the very words he had just spoken to the king: "Thus shall it be done for the man whom the king wishes to honor" (6:11). Haman's plan backfires—180 degrees.

At the level of plot, this change of affairs stands out for several reasons. First, the narrator stops short of describing Haman's inner life during the procession through the open square. He leaves it to the reader to imagine Haman's thoughts of surprise and consternation. Second, Mordecai, who is now bedecked with royal attire, is wearing clothes that are the direct counterpart of his torn clothes and sackcloth that he donned in 4:1. Third, Haman unwittingly devises a plan to honor Mordecai. This motif will surface again when Haman unwittingly builds gallows for himself. Haman has now begun to fall. The wearing of the king's clothes and trappings he had hoped for are given instead to Mordecai in this scene that foreshadows the transfer of power.

One might also be reminded of the writer's ability as an artist in this short passage. Much action is conveyed by repetition, but also by silence. Haman requests that the honoree be given robes, a horse, and a ride through the city with the chauffeur shouting a proclamation (6:7-9). The narrator repeats all of these requests in 6:11 when a summary statement, "So Haman obeyed the king's orders," might have been used. Thus, from the reader's side, Mordecai's reception of the royal gifts takes the form of informational redundancy. Silence also abounds: the person's identity whom the king wishes to honor is kept from Haman until after he describes the ceremony; Ahasuerus knows nothing about the conflict between Haman and Mordecai; Haman has schemed to execute Mordecai along with every other Jew in the kingdom; Mordecai has been working with Esther to save his life and the life of his people. Indeed, the speakers work with different goals in mind and from different sets of assumptions, and the silence that ensues as Haman begins leading Mordecai through the open square contrasts with the previously quoted speech between Haman and the king.

The plot and imagery of 6:8-11 work like literary threads that have already been woven through the story. Like Mordecai, who receives lavish gifts without asking in 6:8-11, Esther expressed no desire to be made queen, nor did she request the cosmetic treatment or any of the "extras" that were hers for the asking (2:13, 15). By contrast, the scene from 6:8-11 might also remind the reader of the first chapter where Vashti refused to dress up royally and be displayed beside pieces of royal property before "the peoples and the officials" (1:11). And finally, these royal robes (*levush malekut*) in 6:8 will also be mentioned again. In 8:15, Mordecai goes out from the presence of the king, this time wearing royal robes of "blue and white," the same colors that had been used to describe the curtains in the opening scene at 1:6.[12] In 6:11 Mordecai is led by someone else, and he wears new clothes. But only for a short time. When he appears in royal garb again in 8:15, he is at this stage obviously a changed man. The near victim issues an edict with full royal authority. Mordecai now looks and acts like a king—or at least a prime minister.

This literary clothes motif is also found outside Esther. Sandra Beth Berg has called attention to the verbal correspondence between the elevation of Joseph and Mordecai. Gen 41:42-43 includes the following description:

> and he arrayed . . . and had him ride . . . and they cried out before him. . . . Then Pharaoh transferred his ring . . . and set it on Joseph's hand.

Esth 6:11 and 8:2 provide a virtual verbatim parallel:

> and he arrayed . . . and had him ride . . . and he cried out before him. . . . Then the king transferred his ring . . . and gave it to Mordecai (Berg 1979:124; cf. also Gan 1961-1962: 144-49).[13]

To this Genesis-Esther parallel Michael Fox adds that the scenes from Esther not only duplicate action from the Joseph narrative, but allow us to glimpse the more lavish, extravagant, and greedy Haman when we compare the two protagonists:

> Instead of Joseph's linen garment and gold necklace, Haman prescribes a garment the king has worn (Joseph also gets the royal signet, but Haman already has this). Instead of Joseph's ride in the viceroy's chariot, Haman wants a ride on the king's horse, with the horse itself bedecked in splendor. Instead of the simple call, "*abrekh*" (an exclamation of obscure derivation), Haman would have himself acclaimed by the cry, "Thus shall it be done for the man whom the king desires to honor!" On top of all this, Haman specifies that the man leading the horse be a nobleman—unwittingly making his own rank a qualification for the role that will humiliate him (1991:76-77).

The King's Scepter and Ring

Two other items that are part of the king's royal attire are his scepter and ring. The golden scepter is mentioned once by

Esther (4:11) and three times by the narrator (5:2 [twice]; 8:4). It functions as a protection device for the king: would-be-visitors, wife included, may approach the king only if he expresses his favor by extending the golden scepter. A few centuries later, Josephus will describe the danger of approaching kings unsummoned. He writes that guards with axes stood by the king's throne for the purpose of cutting down anyone who approached without permission (Fox 1991:208 n. 9). When the scepter is mentioned in 5:2, the queen wins the king's favor and is granted permission to approach, though she apparently would have spoken to him even if the scepter had not been extended (4:16). In another passage, it functions more as a symbol of goodwill or encouragement than as a sign of clemency (8:4). At 8:3 Esther falls at the king's feet weeping and pleading on behalf of her people, but she is already making supplication of the king when he extends the scepter to her.

The other item of the king's garment apparatus, more important for our discussion of the literary carnivalesque because of the role it plays in reversal scenes, is the ring. The ring, like the scepter, is a symbol of extraordinary power. It is used to seal the king's official documents, and, when transferred to someone else, it gives the person virtually full authority for implementing decrees. (Haman's power is held in check to some degree because he apparently must ask permission of the king before hanging Mordecai on the gallows in 6:4.) The ring is mentioned on six separate occasions (3:10, 12; 8:2, 8 [twice], 10). In 3:10 the king takes his ring off and gives it to Haman, and this scene anticipates the second edict that will be sealed, just as the first one was, with the king's ring.[14] In 8:2, the king retrieves the ring and gives it to Mordecai. In both instances, the king makes a big concession because the ring does not merely symbolize the office as the royal robes do (6:8; 8:15): it confers authority.

In the first ring-bestowing episode, Haman gains power to do with the Jews as he desires. The king gives Haman the ring; instructs him to do as he wishes with the "certain people scattered and separated among the peoples" (3:8); then, after the pogrom edict is written in the name of the king, it is sealed with his ring (3:10-12). In the parallel passage of chapter 8, one notices a reversal with variations. In the second ring-transfer scene, the reversal is accentuated by the reference to Haman and his possessions, which have now been given to Esther and Mordecai. The second scene is not just about Ahasuerus who rewards Mordecai with the high position and presents. Mordecai is, after all, deserving: he brought the plot against the king's life to the king's attention (2:21-22). The author also conveys that it is Haman's former position of power that Mordecai is now receiving.

The narrator reports at 8:1 that the king gives Esther Haman's house. Then in 8:2 the king takes off his ring, "which he had taken from Haman," and gives it to Mordecai. Esther in turn gives Mordecai (lit., "sets him over") Haman's house. In the first scene it is the narrator who twice reports the transfer of the ring (3:10, 12). In the second instance, the double reference is found again, but after the narrator's report in 8:2, a second report comes from none other than Ahasuerus himself:

> See, I have given Esther the house of Haman, and they have hanged him on the gallows, because he plotted to lay hands on the Jews. You may write as you please with regard to the Jews, in the name of the king, and seal it with the king's ring; for an edict written in the name of the king and sealed with the king's ring cannot be revoked (8:7-8).

The second scene thus features Mordecai, who apparently is summoned to the king's palace and will soon receive gifts, but only because he is Esther's cousin. Mordecai now has in his possession the same ring, and hence the same power, that Haman once had. Yet the scene in chapter 8 is unlike the one in chapter 3 in an important respect. By introducing Esther, who "set[s] Mordecai over the house of Haman" (8:2), the author highlights her important position in the transfer of power. She, once a powerless virgin, summoned to Susa and given the twelve-month cosmetic treatment, was led to the king's bedroom. Now in chapter 8 she, the one who has no counterpart in the episode of chapter 3, has position, power, and influence in this male-dominated world.

This scene moves from the granting of authority on Esther

and Mordecai to the transfer of the wealth and ring from their enemy, and on to Ahasuerus's injunction to Esther and Mordecai to write their own edicts and to seal them with the king's ring. In both scenes, the one who receives the ring is told to write "as it is good in your [singular in the first instance, plural in the second] eyes" (3:11; 8:8). Both Haman and Mordecai-Esther are allowed to write what seems good to them into law, but such decrees will officially become "the word of the king" only when issued subsequently in the citadel of Susa (3:15; 8:14).

When Esther finds herself speaking again to Ahasuerus face to face in chapter 8, the situation is just as delicate as before (5:1-8; 7:1-9). She begins with a series of conditional clauses ("If it pleases the king" + "If I have won his favor" + "If the thing seems right before the king and I have his approval") as a prelude to her central concern in 8:5. She does request a complete reversal ("let an order be written to revoke the letters devised by Haman . . . which he wrote giving orders to destroy the Jews"), but she certainly does not want to bring up the decree "written in the name of King Ahasuerus and sealed with the king's ring" as the narrator had previously (3:12). So she asks the king for an order "to revoke (*hashiv*) the letters devised by Haman" that called for the destruction of the Jews. The king does not say No to her request. In fact, his response to Esther sounds like a Yes, even in a superlative sense: "See, I have given Esther the house of Haman, and they have hanged him on the gallows, because he plotted to lay hands on the Jews" (8:7). Esther, you've got Haman's house, and what's more, your enemy is now a dead man. And, as if this were not enough, Ahasuerus continues, "You [plural, again Esther and Mordecai] may write as you please with regard to the Jews, in the name of the king, and seal it with the king's ring; for an edict written in the name of the king and sealed with the king's ring cannot be revoked" (8:8). But the reference to the ring and the irrevocable law works in two directions simultaneously. They may write as they "please," but what would please them most, they cannot write precisely because the edict calling for their destruction and the destruction of their people was earlier written and sealed with the king's ring! On the other hand, the king's words might suggest some hope. The new edict they write will also be irrevocable. David Clines's comments on Ahasuerus's double talk deserves to be quoted in toto:

> Esther and Mordecai have only to dictate a letter, it seems, and the deed of Haman will be undone, his letters will be revoked, just as Esther had requested (8.5), and the new decree of revocation will carry permanent and irreversible royal authority. But, on the other hand, those very last words of the sentence, 'cannot be revoked' (*'en lehashiv*), as they sink into the consciousness, renew the tension all over again. For, with the best will in the world, the king has brought into the open his powerlessness to do what Esther has asked; the first decree perfectly fulfilled the conditions for legal irreversibility: written in the king's name, sealed with the king's ring (3.12). The perfect freedom that the first half of the verse has ostensibly granted is severely limited—on this occasion, fatally limited, so it would seem—by the reminder the second half gives of the restricted area within which that freedom may operate. Write what you like, says the king, as long as it doesn't overturn, revoke, or contradict anything previously written. Write what you like to Jewish advantage, says the king, as long as you realize that Haman's decree still stands. Write what you like, says the king, it will bear my seal; but remember that so does every other official document, including Haman's letter. Write what you like, says the king, for I give up; the conundrum of how to revoke an irrevocable decree, as you, Esther have asked, is beyond me; but feel free to write what you like—if you can think of a way to reverse the irreversible (Clines 1984:18-19).

The king thus reveals in his response to her pointed appeal—"How can I bear to see the destruction of my kindred?" (8:6)—that he will not, indeed cannot, grant Esther's request this time. Even in this carnival world, so filled with turnabouts, the irreversible law must stand. Whatever is written as law and sealed with the royal ring cannot be revoked, but we will soon learn that Esther and Mordecai—and not Ahasuerus—do in fact succeed in overcoming Haman's decree in this story (8:8-14). Their decree, which allows the Jews to assemble and defend themselves, has the effect of canceling the planned pogrom.

From this discussion of the king's ring, we turn next to consider an important, and perhaps universal, carnival image: the crown.

THE CARNIVALESQUE: CROWNINGS AND UNCROWNINGS

Crowning already contains the idea of immanent decrowning: it is ambivalent from the very start. . . . Carnival celebrates the shift itself, the very process of replaceability, and not the precise item that is replaced. Carnival is, so to speak, functional and not substantive. It absolutizes nothing, but rather proclaims the joyful relativity of everything.
—Mikhail Bakhtin, *Problems of Dostoevsky's Poetics*

Uncrowning the cathedral bells and hanging them on a horse is a typical carnivalesque gesture of debasement. It combines a destructive theme with that of renewal on another, material bodily level. . . . Church bells, cowbells, and mulebells are to be attached not only to animals but to the beards of the feasting guests. The ringing and jingling of bells is to mark the movement of the munching jaws. It is hard to find an image picturing more strikingly, though coarsely, the logic of abusive uncrowning, destruction and regeneration.
—Mikhail Bakhtin, *Rabelais and His World*

Bakhtin's concept of carnival is based on a folkloric, communal vision of life where folk culture finds itself on the crossroads of parody and travesty. A major element of carnival is the obliteration of differences among people that arise from position and wealth, and we have already seen that carnival literature has its own characteristic logic, the logic of inside-out and turnabout, the logic of forms moving from top to bottom and from front to rear. But the most widespread reversal element is the comic crowning and uncrowning. Even more provocative than the change of clothes motif is the transfer of the crown. Indeed, the primary carnivalistic act is the comic crowning and subsequent uncrowning of a carnival king, and this ritual exists in a number of forms in most carnival festivities and carnivalesque writings. The crown becomes such an indispensable element of folk festival and travesty because it is so easily recognized as a symbol of hierarchy. The jester could be proclaimed king as quickly as the bishop or archbishop could be uncrowned at the "feast of fools" (Bakhtin 1984b:81).

This ritual of crowning and uncrowning is dualistically ambivalent. It expresses the inevitability of culture's shifts and changes, and comic crownings and uncrownings are analogues to what Bakhtin calls the Janus faces of the medieval feast:

> The medieval feast had, as it were, the two faces of Janus. Its official, ecclesiastical face was turned to the past and sanctioned the existing order, but the face of the people of the marketplace looked into the future and laughed, attending the funeral of the past and present (1984b:81).

Rabelais himself was influenced by forms and images not only from the popular festival tradition of his time, but from the antique scholarly tradition of the Saturnalia as well, complete with its own rituals of crowning and uncrowning, exaltation and debasement. In Rabelais's story of Gargantua, King Picrochole is uncrowned. His royal robes are removed, and he is clothed in a smock. He's then caught stealing a donkey at a nearby mill, which leads to an immediate thrashing from the miller. The former king eventually becomes a slave. His fate is a common one of the Saturnalia where slaves were sent to the mill for punishment and beaten and forced to tread the millstone.[15]

While it is true that Bakhtin is concerned with imagery, he is not preoccupied with form alone. All of carnival's images, even the most absurd ones like church bells on animals and the beards of feasting guests, are purposefully aimed at destroying established hierarchies. The uncrowning never assumes the character of personal invective; it aims at a higher level, "at bringing down the high and raising up the low, at destroying every nook and cranny of the habitual picture of the world" (Bakhtin 1981:177). Behind the abuses and blows, Rabelais, for example, views the king, the church, or any institution that misuses power as a possible target for mockery and punishment.

Such ceremonies of uncrowning may involve more than the crown itself. Royal attire is sometimes stripped off the king; the crown and other symbols of authority are removed, and—it is important for our study of Esther—the uncrowned king is also ridiculed and beaten. In the Esther narrative, it is Haman, the one who so obviously craves power and position, who is uncrowned. After he loses his chance at the crown he would have (6:6-11), he and his sons are hanged on the gallows (7:10; 9:14). These and other actions at the level of plot reflect literary conventions of the carnivalesque.

ESTHER: CROWNINGS AND UNCROWNINGS

Because the crown is such an important image of the literary carnivalesque we should not be too surprised to find multiple references to crown wearing and crown swapping in the story of Esther. The "crown" is mentioned four times (1:11; 2:17; 6:8; 8:15).[16] The king is never portrayed as wearing it, but the reader has ample opportunity to discover that, with or without the crown, he is the ultimate authority figure in the story. His power is everywhere apparent. *He* is the one who gives a banquet for all his officials and ministers (1:3) as well as a banquet for the people in the citadel of Susa (1:5). *He* commands the seven eunuchs to bring Queen Vashti to him (1:10-11). *He* sends letters to all the provinces declaring that each man shall be master in his own house (1:22). And, of course, these images of chapter 1 are found elsewhere in the story. Haman's seat is placed above all the other officials because Ahasuerus promotes him (3:1). Mordecai is paraded through the streets wearing the king's robes because the king orders it (6:10). Esther, and in turn Mordecai, will receive Haman's house, but only because the king gives it to her (8:1-2). Without any explicit reference to the king wearing a crown, we are left only to assume that he has one.

Crown swapping takes place among other characters in this story. Haman *craves* power more than anyone else, and it is significant that he is never portrayed as wearing a crown. That the crowning-decrowning motif is at work in this story is obvious when we recall that Esther and Mordecai, the folk heroes, are *given* crowns in this story. In fact, the author portrays only the Jewish protagonists, Esther and Mordecai, wearing crowns.

At the end of the second banquet "when the king is merry with wine" (1:10), he orders Vashti to be brought before him and the people "wearing the royal crown" (1:11). This command for her to put on her crown reveals the king's pompous, extravagant, and frivolous nature. Vashti's refusal to bow to the king's command anticipates both her disenthronement and Esther's coronation in chapter 2. Esther is crowned because she, more than all the virgins of the land, pleases the king in bed: "the king loved Esther more than all the other women; of all the virgins she won his favor and devotion, so that he set the royal crown on her head and made her queen instead of Vashti" (2:17). These two crown scenes are linked by common features: first, the woman who wears the crown is the one who pleases the king; second, she can be uncrowned—and is granted no right to appeal—if she does not cater to her husband's desires.

The crown is referred to once again in 6:8 when Haman asks that it be placed on his head, or on the horse's head that he hopes to ride. Both referents (horse and man) are defensible. The Hebrew text seems to suggest that Haman intends a crown on the horse's head, and such an image is not too outlandish in this carnivalesque story if we consider the scene from chapter 3 of Jonah where the animals are ordered to cover themselves with sackcloth and to call out mightily to God (v. 8).[17] The question, however, of who receives the crown in Esth 6:8 should not distract from the main point: *Haman* wants the horse, the robes, the glory, the show, and perhaps the crown also. Even if the crown is intended for the horse, Haman hopes that all *eyes* will *see* him wearing the king's regalia ("conduct the man on horseback") and that all ears will hear about it ("crying out [for all in the city to hear]"). Yet Haman, who is elevated to a high position in 3:1, never receives a crown in the story. His asking for it in 6:8 (either for himself or for the horse) contrasts with the first two references to the crown (1:11; 2:17). The women did not ask for it. In fact, Vashti refused it. Mordecai reveals a strong desire to save his people, but never suggests that he wants a crown or all that it symbolizes. The image of Haman, therefore, grasping and groping for (but not getting) the crown adds to the carnivalesque flavor of this story of crownings and uncrownings. Mordecai, Haman's arch-enemy, does perhaps eventually receive a crown in the scene from chapter 6 as well as the royal robes and mantle of fine linen and purple in 8:15, and any ambiguity over the placement of the crown at 6:8 is resolved by 8:15 where the narrator reports that Mordecai now wears a crown. In fact, he wears "a great golden crown."[18]

While Haman remains without a crown in this story, the author leaves no doubt that he receives a figurative crown. In 3:1-2 he is promoted above all the officials, after which we learn that the king also commands others to bow down to Haman (3:2b). When one man refuses, there is what appears to be a crushing defeat for that man and all his people. The scene ends with the king and Haman sitting down for cocktails (3:15). In this chapter we see Haman at his high position of power in the story. His rapid ascent is matched by his pride and tendency to brag. It is precisely because one man refuses to bow to Haman that life threatening consequences ensue. Haman delights in telling his wife and friends about "the splendor of his riches, . . . all the promotions with which the king had honored him, and how he had advanced him above the officials and the ministers and the king" (5:11). Haman is in this way "crowned" so that he may be uncrowned in this carnivalesque story.

In light of the thesis that the story of Esther is an early example of the literary carnivalesque, it is not surprising that from chapter 4 on, the turnabouts for Haman (i.e., his fall) and for Esther and Mordecai (i.e., their ascent) are brought about by a concentration of images, including the crown, and the place where it rests, the head. After Haman parades Mordecai through the streets, he hurries home, mourning "with his head covered" (6:12). Two verses later we discover that he has reason to mourn because he, the one who has manipulated the king and who hopes "to destroy, to kill, and to annihilate all Jews" (3:13), is losing control of his own destiny. In 6:14 it appears that Esther is now in a better position than Haman. He is hurried off to the banquet that she has prepared. He will soon find himself on her couch begging for his life. In chapter 7 the king will order the noose to be placed around Haman's neck (v. 9), and his ten sons will suffer the same fate (9:14). Finally, the narrator concludes the description of Haman's fate by pointing out that "the wicked plot . . . should come upon his own *head*" (9:25; emphasis added).

THE CARNIVALESQUE AND MASKS

This is why the mask is so important . . . . The medieval feast, like the ancient carnival, has two faces. The mask of carnival is the aspect of Janus: "Its official, ecclesiastical face was turned to the past and sanctioned the existing order, but the face of the people of the marketplace looked to the future and laughed, conscious it was attending the funeral of the past and present."
—Katerina Clark and Michael Holquist, *Mikhail Bakhtin*

Masks are linked to the public square and the trappings of the theater, and they are an important part of the literary carnivalesque because they are rooted deep in folk traditions. They symbolize joyous chaos, mockery, but, most importantly, play. The mask was once an important symbol for folk culture because it symbolized change and regeneration while concurrently rejecting the image of "conformity to oneself" (Bakhtin 1984b: 39-40). Masks are also symbols of ambiguity itself, of identities that, unmasked, would be monolithic and too often serious. Masks help produce a climate of wonderful relativity during carnival. They may suggest either a grave or a joyous mood, but, by themselves, they do not suggest anything ugly or appalling. Masks are worn both by official priests as well as by unofficial clowns, and, in the Esther narrative, we shall notice that characters in both official and unofficial culture wear masks—though for different reasons.

Bakhtin insists on identifying the mask with a positive vision of reality. After labeling it as the most complex and important element of folk culture, Bakhtin concludes,

the mask is connected with the joy of change and reincarnation, with gay relativity and with the merry negation of uniformity and similarity; it rejects conformity to oneself. The mask is related to transition, metamorphoses, the violation of natural boundaries, to mockery and familiar nicknames. It contains the playful element of life; it is based on a peculiar interrelation of reality and image, characteristic of the most ancient rituals and spectacles (1984b:39-40).

The importance of the mask lies in its intricate symbolism and its peculiar relationship between reality and artistic representation. After the Renaissance, masks became mere symbols of secret identity, signs of social guessing games. They acquired this meaning while retaining some of the features which tied them to folk culture: "the mask hides something, keeps a secret, deceives. . . . The Romantic mask loses almost entirely its regenerating and renewing element and acquires a somber hue. A terrible vacuum, a nothingness lurks behind it" (1984b:40). But during the time of carnival, the mask is consistently associated with folly and carnivalesque glee, and when the fool and the clown put on the mask, carnivalesque authors acquire certain rights: the right to confuse, the right to hyperbolize life, the right to act out life as comedy, the right to rage at official and oppressive culture, and the right to parody others.

ESTHER AND MASKS

In the story of Esther, masks take the form of secrets. Indeed, the tangled webs of the plot are the direct result of discrepancies in awareness between audience and characters on the one hand, and characters and characters on the other. For example, the king does not know that his wife's life is threatened by an edict that he has directed! We know that Mordecai and Esther are cousins and we know of their private conversations, but neither Haman nor Ahasuerus knows what we have been told. And Haman certainly knows that Mordecai's life is in jeopardy, but has no idea that the planned pogrom threatens Esther's life. The scene at 7:3-6 is crucial in this unfolding drama of secrecy because at this point of the narrative both Haman and Esther are unmasked in the king's presence:

> Then Queen Esther answered, "If I have won your favor, O king, and if it pleases the king, let my life be given me—that is my petition—and the lives of my people—that is my request. For we have been sold, I and my people, to be destroyed, to be killed, and to be annihilated. . . ." Then King Ahasuerus said to Queen Esther, "Who is he, and where is he, who has presumed to do this?" Esther said, "A foe and enemy, this wicked Haman!"

This scene deserves our attention, but first let us look at the "masking" scenes that precede it.

Haman wears a mask of secrecy and duplicity in the king's presence at 3:8-9. He tells Ahasuerus, "There is a certain people scattered and separated among the peoples in all the provinces of your kingdom; their laws are different from those of every other people, and they do not keep the king's laws, so that it is not appropriate for the king to tolerate them. . . ." (3:8). Of course, *the* problem is not with "a certain people" or even with their laws. *Haman's* problem is with "a certain man" who will not give him the recognition and honor he craves. Haman carefully considers what to say as he masks his thoughts with words. What he would have the king think is not that this is a plan to help Haman get what Haman wants, but one that will protect the kingdom from an alleged threat of a lawless people. The plan carries the added bonus of enriching the coffers of the king ("I will pay ten thousand talents of silver into the hands of those who have charge of the king's business, so that they may put it into the king's treasuries" [3:9]). Haman thus hides his intentions under the cover of concern for the king and the kingdom.

Haman's veiled reference to the Jews as "a certain people" is, of course, intentional. He wagers that the more depersonalized the victims are, the more likely Ahasuerus will endorse the plan. As Fox notes, "It is easier to kill an abstraction than a person" (1991:48). The phrase "a certain people" might also be translated "a single people." It is, Haman wants to emphasize, only one of a vast number of peoples living in the land, and, what's more, they are "scattered and separated." They will not—Haman would have the king believe—even be missed. It also appears that Haman is forcing a prejudice. The book itself does not evince xenophobic tendencies. In fact, when the letters are dispersed throughout the kingdom for commanding all women to give honor to their husbands, they are sent to each province "in its own script and to every people in its own language" (1:22; cf. 3:12; 8:9).

Haman characterizes the people with a number of words ("scattered," "separated among the peoples," "their laws are different," "they do not keep the king's laws"), but the real issue under discussion ("to destroy them") is only one word in the Hebrew (*le'abbedam*). Even the action is, from Haman's mouth, described as passive: "let it be written."[19] Haman, from behind the mask, does not want the king to take an active role in the genocide. "Please allow me to take care of the details when it comes to working out what's best for the kingdom." Haman succeeds in hiding *his* plan of paying Mordecai back by killing the Jews everywhere. Ahasuerus is persuaded: "The money is given to you, and the people as well, to do with them as it seems good to you" (3:11).

Esther also wears a mask of sorts. When she is taken into the custody of Hegai, the eunuch in charge of the women at the palace, the narrator reports (2:10, 20) that Esther does not reveal her "people or kindred" because Mordecai had requested her to keep it secret.[20] We know why Haman wears a mask; he needs to cover over his outlandish plot to kill a people and punish a man who has hurt his feelings. Esther's and Mordecai's motives in wearing a figurative mask are more elusive. At first glance, it might appear that Mordecai urges Esther to conceal her identity because of anti-Semitic (or, more accurately, anti-Jewish) sentiments. Reference is made as late as 9:1 "to the enemies of the Jews," but the author has suggested that most of the story's characters are not anti-Semitic. Indeed, when Mordecai discloses to the king's servants at the gate that he is a Jew they do not react with outrage or malice (3:4) but speak with him "day after day," apparently attempting to convince him to bow to Haman. The king himself is no anti-Semite. When he wishes to honor Mordecai by giving him presents, the king says to Haman, "Take the robes and the horse . . . and do so to the Jew Mordecai" (6:10). The crowd evinces no anti-Jewish sentiment either, but just the opposite. The inhabitants of Susa are first of all "thrown into confusion" when the pogrom edict is issued (3:15). Then when Mordecai leaves the king's presence wearing the royal regalia several chapters later, he is greeted by the people of Susa with shouts of rejoicing (8:15). Hatred for the Jews in this story is not global, but individual. The plot against the Jews is Haman's and Haman's alone (3:8-9). The narrator does call him "the enemy of the Jews" (3:10) and the plural reference to "the enemies of the Jews" in 9:1 appears to be to any others who might have joined, wittingly or unwittingly, the plot that Haman devised.[21]

Immediately before describing Haman as "the enemy of the Jews" in 3:10, the narrator provides genealogical information. Haman is the son (i.e., descendant) of Hammedatha the Agagite.[22] The problem between Haman and Mordecai is not just personal; it is ancestral. The author provides us with genealogical information about Mordecai. He is son (i.e., descendant) of Jair son of Shimei son of Kish (2:5). Kish was the father of Saul (1 Sam 9:1-2). By mentioning that Haman is a descendant of Agag on five occasions[23] and establishing that Mordecai is a descendant of Saul early in the story, the author places 1 Samuel 15 in the background of the unfolding plot in Esther. The Amalekites had attacked Israel as they made their way from Egypt to Canaan (Exod 17:8-16). Saul later fights Agag, king of the Amalekites, but fails to execute him despite Samuel's explicit instructions to follow the rules of the ban and utterly destroy all of the Amalekites, Agag included. From the Samuel narrator's point of view, the action is repayment for what the Amalekites did to Israel after the exodus (1 Sam 15:2). After a series of denials, Saul finally admits having failed to carry out the ban, and Samuel executes Agag (1 Sam 15:24, 30, 33). Seen against such a backdrop, the ancestral references in Esther make it clear that any friction between the Jew Mordecai and the Gentile Haman have deep roots reaching back to the beginning of Israel's monarchy and even further to the wilderness wanderings.[24] Michael Fox, commenting on 3:3-4, says it well when he writes, "The background reasoning must have gone something like this: 'I cannot bow to Haman because I am a Jew and he is my ancestral enemy. I must not be forced to violate my ethnic sensibility'" (1991:46). From Mordecai's perspective, Haman is not so much a Gentile as an Agagite. Anti-Semitism may not be widespread in Susa, but Mordecai knows that, with an Agagite at court, it pays to be cautious. He does not conceal his Jewish identity from the king's servants at the gate when they urge him to bow to Haman, but he does instruct his cousin Esther to wear her mask (2:10, 20). Only as the plot unfolds do we learn that Mordecai asks Esther to conceal her "people or kindred" so that they would not be utterly destroyed. So, unlike the dim-witted Ahasuerus and egomaniac Haman, Mordecai is anticipating

114

a problem in chapter 2 before it surfaces in chapter 3.

As Mordecai instructs Esther to wear a (figurative) mask, the reader has an opportunity to form impressions about her character. Esther is obedient. In taking Mordecai's words to heart, she provides a contrast to Vashti who, in the opening chapter, did not listen—and for good reason—to her husband. The action in the opening scenes leads to the drafting of a farcical law issued to ensure that men would be masters of their households. Esther's obedience at 2:10—and the narrator will mention it again at 2:20—is of course not motivated by any imperial law. She, in her wisdom, takes Mordecai's commands to heart, and she will subsequently instruct him: "Go, gather all the Jews to be found in Susa, and hold a fast on my behalf, and neither eat nor drink for three days, night or day. I and my maids will also fast as you do" (4:16). Mordecai follows her instructions to the letter. He "did *everything* as Esther had ordered him" (4:17; emphasis added). Obedience will become an issue again at 4:8 when Mordecai will command Esther just as he had at 2:10 and 2:20. His command at 4:8 precipitates Esther's unmasking. Mordecai "charges her to go to the king to make supplication to him and entreat him for her people" (4:8).

The conversation between Queen Esther and King Ahasuerus in 7:2-6, the grand unmasking scene, is important in this discussion of carnivalesque masks because Esther brings information out in the open that has thus far been kept secret at the palace. Readers and characters travel different paths toward enlightenment as information in the story is disclosed. We know that Haman devises a plan to kill all the Jews, and, when he later boasts before his friends and his wife ("Even Queen Esther let no one but myself come with the king to the banquet that she prepared. Tomorrow also I am invited by her" [5:12]), we may anticipate what Haman does not even suspect: His days may be numbered. Ahasuerus is even more in the dark. He does not know that his wife is Jewish, and he also has no idea that his endorsement of Haman's plan threatens her life. With Esther, Ahasuerus, and Haman together in the climactic scene of chapter 7, with secrets abounding, with the threat of death weighing heavily on Esther, and with Esther hinting that her mind is made up (4:16), all the conditions appear to have been met for a grand unmasking.

This unmasking scene allows us to see Esther as an intelligent woman in her own right, and her brilliance is made even more apparent by the dim-witted king and prime minister who stand nearby. (The "fool" is an important character in the literary carnivalesque and is discussed in the next chapter.) After two preliminary "if" clauses in 7:3 ("if I have won your favor" and "if it pleases the king"), Esther gets right to the point. These banquets I've been giving and the promises you've been making all lead to this one request: Let my life be given me. You asked for my petition. This is it. And also, I would like to ask that the lives of my people be spared. After making the request—and as she explains it, it certainly seems modest—she quickly provides the justification: "For we have been sold, I and my people, to be destroyed, to be killed, to be annihilated." The words in the three-pronged repetition had appeared in Haman's original genocidal edict (3:13), but now they ring in the king's ears with a different contextual nuance. One person who will be "destroyed, killed, and annihilated" is none other than the king's wife. But Esther doesn't stop here. To make her point even more convincing, she suggests hypothetically that she could have kept this a secret *if* she and her people had been sold "merely as slaves." If I had been a mere slave, Esther tells her husband, I would have been silent "for then the adversity would not have justified causing loss to the king" (Fox's translation 1991:82). A key word, *shavah*, appears in Esther's final clause. It suggests "being in the best interest," "justification for," or "equal to." In other words, Esther gambles and makes an appeal for what she thinks will cause her husband to join her side. My life is not the issue, she says, not even the lives of my people. My request is what's in the best interest of the kingdom. Killing people in your kingdom is not such a good idea. (Recall that Haman had tried to downplay the projected massacre: these people are scattered, separated, law breakers, and people who should not be tolerated [3:8].) Esther's point is that "the enemy of the Jews" is also the king's enemy. Of course, Esther had not been present when Haman presented the plan to the king in chapter 3. But the narrator has her use the same key word, *shavah* (a word used infrequently in the Hebrew Bible), that Haman had spoken in 3:8. So the narrator hints that Esther can play the same game—even using some of the same words— that Haman did. Her strategy for convincing the king is not unlike Haman's. Both appeal to what they hope will be inter- preted as in the king's best interest. You've promised *me* half the kingdom, but my only request is for you to do what's best for *your* kingdom, Esther would have the king believe.

The king expresses his outrage in two questions in 7:5: Who is he? And where is he? Maybe Ahasuerus is distancing himself from the crime. Esther was cleverly ambiguous and careful not to point a finger at the king, though she did at least hint that Ahasuerus was responsible for this crisis when she said, "We've been sold." It is, however, not inconceivable that Ahasuerus's memory fails him. The narrator has provided several clues to suggest his below average intelligence. The king's *carte blanche* given to Haman ("Do with [the Jews] as it seems good to you" [3:11]) certainly suggests that he is not all that interested either in the plan or its execution. His pointed questions now in 7:5 also create some ambiguity about his point of view. Perhaps he is outraged because someone threatens Esther's well being and the well being of her people, but the narrator leaves open the possibility that he may be concerned because *his* royal honor has been threatened.

When Esther speaks to the king, she does not mention Haman's name. She creates a situation whereby the king be- comes angry and then asks to know who is and where is the culprit. The response that the unmasking provokes is reminis- cent of the opening scene when the former queen refused her husband publicly. Little does the king know that he is once again being undone in his own house.

In response to the king's two questions, Esther supplies a two part answer: "A foe and enemy" and "this wicked Haman" (7:6). She not only identifies the villain; she also characterizes him. Esther could answer straightforwardly: Who is he: Haman. Where is he: Right here. But with her husband obviously out- raged, she is shrewd enough to say what needs be said now that Haman's mask is slipping, rather than to respond with simple answers to the questions at hand.[25] Her response to her husband's questions certainly has a "he is the man" kind of quality about it, reminiscent of Nathan's stinging rebuke of David after the parable of the poor man's ewe lamb (2 Sam 12:7). But along with Esther's accusation are the accompanying words "foe," "enemy," and "wicked."

After the dialogue, the narrator resumes the storytelling and informs us that "Haman was terrified" and that "the king rose from the feast in wrath and went to the palace garden" (7: 6b-7a). Neither the description of Haman's inner world ("terrified") or outer world ("rose and went") is surprising. Haman certainly has reason to be terrified, and the king is by this stage famous for indecisiveness. He's buying time here just as in the past when faced with a crisis. Several actions sanctioned by the king transpire in this story, but the narrator goes to some length to let us know that the plans are often made by someone other than the king. Memucan devises the plan that is supposed to cause women to honor their husbands (1:16-21), and Haman is obviously responsible for planning the pogrom (3:6-11). Now Ahasuerus finds himself in his own house facing a dilemma once again. "He is going outside," David Clines observes, "because he is going to have to choose between his prime minister, whom he himself has publicly promoted (3.1), and his queen, a girl of uncertain ancestry who has nothing much to recommend her except her good looks and her cookery" (1984:15).

In this scene in chapter 7, the king is portrayed again as taking little initiative in resolving the crisis. In fact, it is Haman who seals his own fate. The king is outside in the palace garden, and Esther and Haman are alone for the first (and only) time in the story. Haman quickly "throws himself on the couch where Esther was reclining" (v. 8). The passage is charged with irony. In this compromising position, Haman appeals to one whose life the edict threatens. The appeal to Esther is also ironically charged in another sense. Haman has threatened Esther's life; he's only threatened the king's honor. Why not appeal to the king? The narrator appears to suggest that Haman is not only desperate, but suspects perhaps that the king would be more threatened by losing face than by losing his wife. It is not the king, but Harbona, one of the eunuchs, who suggests a way to resolve the crisis: "Look, the very gallows that Haman has prepared for Mordecai, whose word saved the king, stands at Haman's house." The observation prompts Ahasuerus: "Hang him on that" (v. 9). Notice that it is not the edict that causes the king to turn against his own prime minister. What settles the issue is Ahasuerus's mistaken notion that the queen is being assaulted ("Will he even assault the queen in my presence, in my own house?" [v. 8]). Ahasuerus does not bother to call Esther's name here. She is "the queen." He is obviously more concerned with what *he* perceives is being done to the queen, *his* wife, than with Esther herself. "In my presence," "in the palace," he exclaims. With Haman's mask down, the king is outraged. How dare he do that *here*!

5

PARODY

THE CARNIVALESQUE:
DEATH, DYING, AND "PREGNANT DEATH"

In the process of destroying an old hierarchical picture of the world, Rabelais put a new one in its place. He reevaluated death itself, and, by putting death in the here and now world, he affirmed that it was an inescapable part of life itself (Bakhtin 1981:193). Death is not merely negative; it is instead ambivalent. "Birth is fraught with death, and death with new birth," Bakhtin writes in *Problems of Dostoevsky's Poetics* (1984a:125), and a central carnival image is what he calls "pregnant death." Death takes the form of renewal, a combination of death and rebirth, and carnival's abusive expressions "always contain in some topographical and bodily aspect the image of pregnant death" (1984b:352).

Death plays an important part in the imagery system of Rabelais's *Gargantua and Pantagruel*, and one of the main themes of the novel is that of birth-giving death. When Pantagruel, so huge and heavy, is born in Book 2 Chapter 2, he suffocates his mother, Badebec. Gargantua, father of the newborn Pantagruel, finds himself in an awkward situation. When the mother of the newborn Pantagruel dies, the narrator reports that Gargantua does not know whether to weep or laugh:

> [Gargantua] was at a complete loss what to say or do. A terrible doubt racked his brain: should he weep over the death of his wife or rejoice over the birth of his son? . . . "Shall I weep?" he cried. . . . "[Yes,] because my dear wife is dead!" . . . As he spoke, he cried like a cow. But suddenly, struck by the thought of Pantagruel, he began to laugh like a calf (Rabelais 1936:173-74).

Unable to resolve the doubt, Gargantua weeps and laughs, and this ambiguity has implications on a much larger scale. The entire carnivalesque world is portrayed as giving birth and regenerating death. Death is viewed "not as part of an all-encompassing temporal sequence but rather as something on the boundary of time, not *in* a life series but at the edge of that series" (Bakhtin 1981:193; original emphasis).

With respect to the story of Esther, Bakhtin's most important argument about death is his point that death manifests itself as utter annihilation when viewed from an individual perspective, but when viewed from the community's perspective it becomes part of a life-giving cycle whereby the community survives. The story of Esther stands as a symbol of hope for a people in the face of persecution. Folk culture's encounter with death is linked to the festive occasion itself. It is this communal sense that forms the heart of joyous festivities and celebration of change and renewal. The shouting, celebrating, and feasting reflected in the final chapters of Esther are all symbolic actions of life's triumph over death that purge the community of violence and destruction in carnivalesque literature. Death offers the greatest challenge to celebration, but it also becomes the necessitating force, the driving force *for* celebration. Always ambiguous, death is what is most celebrated against. It is for this reason that festivity, in literature such as the Esther story, plays such an important role in highlighting the carnivalesque concept of death as renewal. Triumph over death requires a recognition of its power and inevitability, but a larger sense of life emerges when the community affirms itself against individual mortality.

ESTHER: DEATH, DYING, AND "PREGNANT DEATH"

We have already observed that 6:13 represents a key turning point in the Esther (M) narrative. In a collective voice, Zeresh and Haman's advisers say to him, "[You] will surely fall before him." The pronouns highlight the turn of events: "You" now refers to Haman and not to Mordecai as the plot had led us to expect all along. "Him" applies to Mordecai and not to "the enemy of the Jew" as the sequence of events had suggested. Several of the key points in the narrative where the motif of

imminent death is apparent before 6:13 have also been discussed. It may be helpful to summarize these events quickly
before looking more carefully at the concentration of life and
death sequences that surface after 6:13.

The motif of imminent death does not surface explicitly in
chapter 1, but it certainly lurks beneath the surface. After Vashti
refuses to appear before the king and his guests, she is banished
and will one day be replaced: "Vashti is never again to come
before King Ahasuerus; and let the king give her royal position
to another who is better than she" (v. 19). This retaliatory action is aimed at one person, Vashti, but has implications for everyone in the kingdom: "so when the decree made by the king is
proclaimed throughout all his kingdom, vast as it is, all women
will give honor to their husbands, high and low alike" (v. 20).
The action, carried out in accordance with "the laws" of the
land, sets a tone for the events that follow. Indeed, the motif of
imminent death is found explicitly in each of the remaining
chapters.[1] In chapter 2, the eunuchs, Bigthan and Teresh, conspire to assassinate the king, but their plot is spoiled when
Mordecai discloses it to Esther, who in turn discloses it to the
king (vv. 21-22). In chapter 3, Haman plots to kill "*all* the Jews"
after Mordecai refuses to bow (vv. 6-11). In chapter 4 the motif
appears once again. Although Mordecai does not enter the
king's gate dressed in sackcloth, he does approach the entrance
(v. 2). Such action is provocative and possibly dangerous. Later,
when Mordecai urges Esther to approach the king, he speaks to
her by means of a messenger. Esther responds by emphasizing
the peril involved: "all the king's servants and the people of the
king's provinces know that if any man or woman goes to the
king inside the inner court without being called, there is but one
law—all alike are to be put to death" (v. 11). Five verses later,
Esther reveals that she will indeed risk her life. She will go to
the king, even though such action is prohibited by law. Her
words to Mordecai in v. 16, punctuated with a staccato rhythm,
highlight the drama: "if I perish, I perish" (*veka'asher 'avadti
'avadti*). Three days later, in chapter 5, Haman leaves the inner
court of the king's palace after learning that he has been invited
to yet another banquet sponsored by Queen Esther. Swelling

with pride, he shares what he thinks is good news with his wife: "Even Queen Esther let no one but myself come with the king to the banquet that she prepared. Tomorrow also I am invited by her, together with the king" (v. 12). After also revealing that the sight of Mordecai depresses him, Haman's wife and friends give him advice: "Let a gallows fifty cubits high be made, and in the morning tell the king to have Mordecai hanged on it" (v. 14). Mordecai's days are numbered, or so it appears.

Of course, the motif of imminent death appears again in chapter 6, but with a new object: Haman. The turn of events is suggested by the king who first of all orders Haman to give the royal robes to Mordecai in v. 10, and then to show Mordecai off—the king obviously delights in displaying people—by leading him on horseback through the open square. The narrator also shows this change when introducing the quoted speech in v. 13. In the earlier scene, Haman had received advice from his wife and friends. They instructed him to build a gallows and to have Mordecai hanged on it (5:14). This group speaks to him again in chapter 6 after the king reveals his wish to honor Mordecai, but it is no longer his "friends," but his "wise men" and wife Zeresh who give advice (v. 13). In the first passage, his "friends" suggest the plot to execute Mordecai, but the second group, the "wise men," predict Haman's downfall. In a book where ethnicity plays a major part, their words stand out because it is Gentiles who are now predicting a Jewish victory. Even Haman's wife and friends see Jewish victory as inevitable.

Their statement to Haman begins with a conditional clause, "if Mordecai before whom your downfall has begun." The word "if" translates literally the Hebrew 'im, but their statement conveys a sense of inevitability and may also be translated "since . . . ." The prediction that Haman's wife and friends make is, at first glance, unusual. Why do they take Haman's embarrassment as a sign of defeat? After all, his plan to have Mordecai hanged on the gallows is still a secret; Haman has merely been made to robe Mordecai and escort him through the open square. What are we to make of their alarmist response? It appears that Haman's destiny, according to his wife and friends, is guided by something—and they do not call it God—

beyond themselves or this world. They tell him, "if [or: "since"] Mordecai is of the Jewish people," and herein lies a clue. It is Mordecai's Jewishness that somehow foreshadows victory over Haman. According to those who now speak, it is not because Mordecai has power by himself to overcome Haman, but because he is part of an inevitable movement. As Michael Fox notes, Haman's falling has "its own dynamic, a trajectory propelled by a force they do not identify" (1991:80). By viewing Haman's disgrace as a sign of his approaching downfall, they reinforce an idea that Mordecai had already suggested. In an attempt to convince Esther to approach the king on behalf of the Jewish people, Mordecai instructed her, "If you keep silence at such a time as this, relief and deliverance will rise for the Jews from another quarter" (4:14). This quoted speech of Mordecai and of Haman's wife and associates in 6:13 suggests that history is, according to the author, guided. The Jewish people will endure in a world even when events are channeled against them. It is as though Gentiles know in advance, as many readers no doubt would, that Amalek cannot destroy Israel (cf. Exod 17:14-16 and 1 Sam 15). Their words in 6:13 suggest that history is not only foreshadowed, but ethnically predetermined. Haman's "fall," inevitable because Mordecai is a Jew, is emphasized three times in the same verse by the repetition of the Hebrew word *naphal*, which highlights the action itself: "Since your fall has begun, you will fall, you will certainly fall." In the next chapter Haman will indeed *fall* upon Esther's couch just as the king returns to the room. Earlier, Mordecai refused to bow (that is, to fall) to Haman, and ironically, in 7:8, Haman falls before a Jew to plead for his life, as his wife and associates had predicted.

The quoted speech in 6:13 suggests something else. The tale of Esther does not depict Persians as anti-Semites. Haman, like Mordecai and Esther, is a non-Persian,[2] and the counsel he receives in 6:13 is certainly not what one would expect from an anti-Semite's wife. There is plenty of male chauvinism, violence, pomposity, and tantrum throwing displayed in this story, but one looks in vain to find Persians who are anti-Semites.[3] Haman the Agagite is the only character explicitly named "enemy of the Jews" in the story. It is certainly possible that Mordecai does not bow to Haman because Mordecai is a Jew and his faith does not allow it,[4] but *Haman's* anger is not driven by religious or ethnic concerns. This Agagite vents his anger on "all" the Jews because he so despises the non-bowing Mordecai, who happens to be Jewish. For his part, Ahasuerus does not reveal any anti-Jewish sentiment. It is true that he allows Haman to lay plans for the pogrom, but the king is completely unaware of the intended victims. Ahasuerus knows only of "a certain people . . . [whose] laws are different from those of every other people" (3:8). When Esther later reveals that she and her people "have been sold . . . to be destroyed, to be killed, and to be annihilated," the not-fully-informed and ever-forgetful Ahasuerus asks, "Who is he, and where is he, who has presumed to do this?"

THE "MASSACRES" OF CHAPTERS 8 AND 9

The author uses numerous images to convey the death and dying motif, a central image of the literary carnivalesque, throughout this story. But no one is killed until chapter 7. The change from anticipated death to actual death begins at 7:10 when the wicked Haman is hanged on the gallows, and this thematic shift is accentuated in chapters 8 and 9 as thousands of people are massacred. This dramatic shift in tone has occupied a number of commentators, and may be reconsidered in the light of the thesis that the Esther (M) story is an example of early carnivalesque writings. Let us first consider the plot.

Forecast

The catastrophic events of chapters 8–9 fall into two parts. The first is the forecast, where three times the image of death is explicit (8:11-12; 8:13; 9:1), and the second is the enactment (9:5-16). The forecast opens with the new royal law described:

> By these letters the king allowed the Jews who were in every city to assemble and defend their lives, to destroy, to kill, and to annihilate any armed force of any people or province that might attack them, with their children and women, and to plunder their goods on a single day . . . on the thirteenth day of the twelfth month, which is the month of Adar (8:11-12).

This edict is written with the king's full authority (vv. 8-14), and, according to Mordecai's command (v. 9), it permits Jews to defend themselves (or literally, "to stand for their lives").[5] We may assume self-defense to have been illegal according to the terms of the first decree. Esther hopes to "revoke the letters devised by Haman" (v. 5), but what she and Mordecai receive is permission to write a new decree that supplements without cancelling the original one. Since Persian law is irreversible, the law devised by Haman must stand. Esther can only ask for a new edict which allows Jews to defend their lives against any armed force or people "that might attack them" (v. 11).

The call for annihilation of the Jew's enemies is reminiscent of the rules for war during the occupation of Canaan, the time of the Judges, and the early monarchy. But the key word *herem* ("utter destruction") does not appear in Esther, and one other major element is absent: God is not portrayed as waging this war. The familiar three words ("destroy," "kill," "annihilate") are now appearing for the third time (3:13; 7:4; 8:11), and this kind of duplication allows for an observation. Esther used the same three words in 7:4 when she exposed Haman's plan to the king. That is, the author portrays Esther twice using the language of chapter 3 even though she was not privy to the original conversation that took place in the inner circle of power! Her speech, and indeed the forecasted preparations for war in 8:11-13, reflects a literary convention. (We will return to the implications of this concept in a moment.)

Unlike the first decree, 8:11 opens with an important phrase, "the king allowed." The action that the Jews may take will be carried out in a manner consistent with the Persian legal system itself. The king, dim-witted though he is, now has a better understanding of what has taken place under Haman's leadership, and in fact in chapter 9 will ask Esther if anything else can be done. He grants Esther and Mordecai permission to "write as [they] please" in the name of the king and to seal it with the king's ring (v. 8). This forecasted attack, soon to be augmented, is carried out with the king's knowledge and permission.

Esther had originally asked that Haman's edict be rescinded back at 8:5. The action moves to a new level after the king denies her request. The narrator's report of the edict, which is written and sealed, continues in 8:13, and the description is virtually a verbatim parallel of 3:14. The Jews are, however, now identified as those who are to be ready on that day.

> A copy of the writ was to be issued as a decree in every province and published to all peoples, and the Jews were to be ready on that day to take revenge on their enemies (8:13).

The explanatory phrase, "to take revenge on their enemies," also stands out because it has no counterpart in 3:14. The audience hears (or reads) these words now for the first time because Haman's edict did not, and from Haman's perspective should not, call for vengeance. For good reason, Haman keeps his feelings of hatred from Ahasuerus when he makes his case that "a certain people" pose a threat to the kingdom (3:8). Haman is a liar. A certain people pose no such threat; one man threatens another's ego. In a startling departure from the biblical norm, the vengeance forecasted here is not the Lord's, and the phrase appears to shift the emphasis from self-defense (8:11) to an offensive attack. The key word *lehinnaqem* ("to take revenge"), however, always presupposes a wrong action, one group's misguided offense to which another party responds (Fox 1991:101). This "vengeance" is specifically targeted against an actively hostile group. It is not punishment of an unarmed or unsuspecting group for a previous wrong. Neither is it a general license to kill, but is (still) a very specific type of directive that is defensive in nature. The forecasted attack in chapter 8 is directed toward "enemies," "foes," or "those who would attack," as they are repeatedly named by the narrator in chapters 8–9.[6]

The motif of imminent death surfaces once again at 9:1. Though Mordecai has commanded this edict (8:9), the narrator reminds us that it originates with the king:

> when the king's command and edict were about to be executed, on the very day . . . when the Jews would gain power over their foes (9:1).

This final leg of the forecast reintroduces the motif that the fighting will take place against "foes." The narrator has stressed the king's role: It is "the king's secretaries" who write the edict.

It is published "in the name of King Ahasuerus," sealed with "the king's ring," and delivered by horses from the "royal herd." It is by these letters that the "king allowed" the Jews to defend themselves, and so the couriers make haste to spread the word because of the "king's command" (8:9-14). The plan is made and executed according to law, and by this stage of the story we discover that Haman's claim of a people who "do not keep the king's laws" (3:8) is ironically charged.

Enactment

The plot moves logically from forecast to enactment in chapter 9. On the scheduled day of annihilation, 13 Adar, the Jews take the initiative, and the narrator highlights their actions with an abundance of verbal forms in vv. 1-5 ("gathered," "seized," "spread," "grew more powerful," "struck down," "slaughtering," "destroying"). The action may be divided into three parts for the purpose of exposition (vv. 5-10, 11-15, 16).

Michael Fox points out that the issue of control is one of the major themes of the book. The theme appears in the opening chapter when Ahasuerus commands Vashti to parade before the guests. It appears again when the virgins are summoned to the court, when they cater to the king's sexual whims, later when Mordecai refuses to bow to Haman, and when Haman attempts to wipe out all of the Jews (1991:108). The specific form that control takes now in chapter 9 is massacre. The first leg of the enactment sets the tone for an accelerating chain of events:

> So the Jews struck down all their enemies with the sword, slaughtering, and destroying them, and did as they pleased to those who hated them. In the citadel of Susa the Jews killed and destroyed five hundred men. They killed . . . the ten sons of Haman . . . and they did not touch the plunder (vv. 5-10).

Neither the tools of the elaborate state system nor the Jewish queen and prime minister could resolve the crisis. This is a massacre, but a few points should be borne in mind. The action is obviously modeled on a blueprint of turnabout: those who are overcome are the ones who had hoped to gain power (v. 1); the ones slaughtered and destroyed (v. 5) are the ones who had been given permission to slaughter and destroy (3:13). Furthermore, the action in chapter 9 is in response to a planned pogrom against "all Jews." It is *Haman's scheme and inflexible Persian law* that necessitates a war—or is it a war?—against those who would take the initiative. Although the event is reminiscent of the holy war ban,[7] the scene in Esther is not portrayed as a purging or cleansing of the land. Even the forecasted tit-for-tat retribution is cut short in the enactment. The enemies of the Jews had been ordered under Haman's edict to plunder the Jews' goods (3:13), and the motif is repeated in chapter 8. Under the plan that Mordecai commands, the Jews are also given a specific directive to plunder the goods of their attackers. But the author casts the action more narrowly along self-preservation lines in the enactment. In 9:10 (and again in vv. 15, 16) the narrator stresses that the Jews take no plunder. Michael Fox points out that the Jews here are not waging a campaign against "all gentiles." This is not a religious crusade against the heathen or a battle reminiscent of Joshua's conquest of Canaan, nor an imperialist war reminiscent of the days of David, John Hyrcanus, or Alexander Jannaeus (1991: 223). And "there is certainly no need to imagine," LaCocque writes (1987:216), "that a sick mind produced at this juncture the description of a gang-like slaying of innocent people uniquely because they were not Jews."

Another discrepancy between forecast and enactment becomes apparent when we learn in 9:6 that "the Jews killed and destroyed five hundred men (*ish*)," and in 9:15 that "they killed three hundred men (*ish*) in Susa." We had been set up to anticipate a destruction, killing, and annihilation not only of the men, but of children and women as well (8:11). The exclusion of non-combatants, which appears to be the case here, may have been the exception rather than the rule in the ancient Near East. Women, land, and livestock were routinely viewed as the responsibility of and/or the property of men. Thus Fox (1991:225) notes the difference between the battles of Esth 9 and other parts of the Hebrew Bible: "Joshua destroyed Achan's sons and daughters—and livestock and property—along with the guilty man himself (Josh 7:24-25); God obliterated the family (and property) of Korah (Num 16:32); and God commanded the Israelites to exterminate men, women, and children in the conquest of Canaan (Deut 20:16-17; Josh 6:17-24)."

The description of action turns in 9:11 to a vignette between Queen Esther and King Ahasuerus.

> The number of those killed in the citadel of Susa was reported to the king. The king said, ". . . what further is your request? It shall be fulfilled." Esther said, "If it please the king, let the Jews who are in Susa be allowed tomorrow also to do according to this day's edict, and let the ten sons of Haman be hanged on the gallows." So the king commanded this to be done; a decree was issued in Susa. . . . The Jews . . . killed three hundred persons in Susa; but they did not touch the plunder (vv. 11-15).

The scene shows events transpiring, in contrast to the plans that Haman had laid, with the king's full knowledge, and the narrator appears to be stressing the point that Ahasuerus is at the center of the unfolding drama: The news of the massacre is first reported "to the king"; Ahasuerus asks what has been done "in the rest of the king's provinces"; when Esther indicates her request, she prefaces it with "if it pleases the king"; and after she makes her request, "the king commanded this to be done." Now that the masks have dropped, this latest scene is a reversal of Haman's ambiguous and unspecific request ("a certain people . . ."). An ironic point reinforces the change of affairs: in the course of the vignette we learn that, despite Haman's objections, these people *do* keep and abide by the king's laws (cf. 3:8). And finally, as Fox acknowledges (1991:112), the foolhardy king becomes a partisan of the Jews. He appears in this scene to take some credit for the victory when he offers an additional gift, though we know that it is Esther and Mordecai who asked and then wrote as they wished.

Michael Fox views this scene as a "literary flaw" (1991:113), and offers the following explanation for his conclusion. The king's latest offer is here "unexpected and unmotivated" by the story, and the narrative provides no reason to think that Esther desires that any more be done. She has already been given permission to write into law whatever she pleases. Her request, according to Fox, also appears to be unnecessary if it is true that everyone in the kingdom operates in strict accordance with the law, in which case the Jews would not have been threatened under the edict devised by Haman on 14 Adar as they would have on 13 Adar. Finally, this additional day of fighting may have been introduced for etiological reasons—to explain why the Susan Jews celebrate on 15 Adar (9:18). Since Fox is well aware of the book's artistic merit and since he rarely finds any "literary flaws" in the story, his point deserves careful consideration.

I believe the text permits another perspective. Loss of life on 13 Adar is confined to the fortress of Susa. When asked "if more can be done," ever-perceptive Esther may anticipate additional problems from enemies outside the fortress itself, and, therefore, requests permission to continue the war in the *city* of Susa. It is also possible that the reference to this second day of fighting is not etiological as Fox suggests. That is, the feast might be celebrated on 15 Adar because of this extra day of fighting. In addition, the vignette is not inconsistent with the psychological portrayal of the king elsewhere. On several occasions he has catered to Esther and Haman, often invoking profuse language.[8]

> Now the other Jews who were in the king's provinces also gathered to defend their lives, and gained relief from their enemies, and killed seventy-five thousand of those who hated them; but they laid no hands on the plunder (9:16).

The narrator directs us back in time to the previous day, 13 Adar, and shifts attention on the spatial plane to describe events outside Susa. The report of fighting in the provinces duplicates some themes and ideas that had appeared previously: the fighting takes place in the "king's provinces," the "enemy" is overcome, and the plunder is not seized. But the number of victims, more than 90 times greater than the Susan casualty figure of 810, stands out.

If the extra day of fighting in Susa can somehow be explained as a necessity of the plot, surely this new revelation casts the fighting to a new level. Vengeance and bloodthirst deserve our protest. The victims number 75,000 and the attackers escape unscathed. This appears to be overkill. Indeed, the historian might find a parallel in the Allied bombings of Dresden or in the atomic bombs dropped on Nagasaki and Hiroshima. Haman has been identified as an historical figure in this story. He is an "Agagite" and an Amalekite, and, despite the many years that separate the Exodus from the Diaspora, such evil dispositions and designs are still very much alive. The new Amalekite's unjust rage against an individual becomes such a problem that it is elevated to genocidal proportions. The attack outside Susa is in response to a planned pogrom that was written as an irreversible law and sent—as any good historian would report it—"to every province in its own script and every people in its own language . . . calling on all the peoples to be ready for that day" (3:12-14). But is this an historian's account of war?

Chapters 8–9 and the Literary Carnivalesque

As we look closely at these death, dying, or, in Bakhtin's words, "pregnant death" images in the closing chapters, one overarching question arises: How are these killings to be understood if we are correct that this story is part of antiquity's literary carnivalesque? Much has been written about the so-called massacres in chapters 8 and 9 of Esther, but not always with context in mind. One can find "a massacre, a Jewish bloodbath against Persians" (Goldman 1990:24) at the end of the Esther narrative, and the numbers *by themselves*—500+10+300+75,000 without a single Jewish casualty—certainly suggest a bloodletting of epic proportions. I have argued above that such views, indeed all views, are influenced by presuppositions *about* the book, presuppositions which we bring to the story and presuppositions about what the story purports to illustrate and to teach—or not to teach.

Readers correctly perceive that the threat of death in the opening chapters is disproportionately augmented in chapters 8 and 9 where a tone of harsh vengeance and ruthless destruction of the enemy replaces the initial threats. Martin Luther's perspective is famous: "I am so hostile to [2 Maccabees] and to Esther that I could wish that they did not exist at all; for they judaize too greatly and have much pagan impropriety."[9] His sentiment still finds expression today among both Jewish and Christian commentators. Bernhard Anderson voiced a feeling perhaps not too uncommon when we wrote that

> a Christian minister . . . faithful to the context . . . will not take
> [a] text from Esther; and, if the leader of a church-school class
> shows any Christian discernment, he [or she] will not waste
> time trying to show that the heroes of the book are models of
> character, integrity, and piety.[10]

Claude Montefiore, a Jewish scholar of biblical and rabbinic
Judaism, expressed his view in his once popular book, *The
Bible for Home Reading*. Objecting to the nationalistic overtones
of the book and what he viewed as disproportionate revenge
enacted by the Jews, Montefiore wrote:

> We can hardly dignify or extenuate the operations of the Jews
> by saying that they were done in self-defence. For we are told
> that all the officials helped the Jews, and that none durst
> withstand them. Moreover, the slaying apparently[11] included
> both women and children. . . . [The narrator reports] a massa-
> cre of unresisting Gentiles (1899:403).

Montefiore also discovers in the book of Esther, which he "cannot regard . . . as divine or inspired," a tone of "cruelty and of
revenge," especially in the "last pages [that] reek with blood"
(1899:405).

Several attempts have been made to "overcome" the problems. The reference in the forecast to killing "children and
women" (8:11) is excessive to some commentators (Fox 1991:
224), and Robert Gordis has made a valiant effort to diminish
the perceived ethical problem of allowing them to be massacred.
He translates the phrase in question in this way: "and wipe out
every armed force of a people or a province attacking them,
their children, and their wives" (1976:51-52). Gordis understands the "children and women" as possible Jewish *victims* in
the forecasted battle, but his translation is unconvincing for two
reasons: first, the Hebrew simply does not allow it, as Fox
(1991:284-85) has demonstrated; second, these instructions and
the dispatch of the letter in 8:9-14 obviously parallel 3:12-15.
The call to attack women and children and to plunder their
goods is duplicated—that is, merely duplicated—from 3:13.

Attempts have also been made to overcome the perceived
ethical or moral problem by another route. S. Talmon (1963:
419-55), for example, points out that this call for total destruc-

tion of soldiers and families is entirely consistent with the wisdom doctrine of retributive justice. Haman and any of his supporters are to receive nothing less that what they had intended to give, and, Talmon suggests, the book of Esther is part of the wisdom tradition. But there are a few shortcomings with this interpretation. Wisdom is an encompassing term that can be used to designate almost any book or portion of the Hebrew Bible, and, in the story of Esther, the author portrays only one man plotting against all the Jews of Persia. The context for interpreting this passage must extend well beyond the tradition of wisdom literature.

The book's "imperfections" in the final chapters have been explained in another manner. In a provocative, cogently argued book, *The Esther Scroll: The Story of a Story*, David J. A. Clines advances the view that at an early phase the Masoretic story of Esther reached its conclusion at the end of chapter 8. He "reconstruct[s] a . . . genesis and history for the Esther story" (1984:50), but without neglecting—and in this way his contribution is exceptional—the literary contours of the book. His theory explains the "problems" at the book's terminus by positing that the

> author of ch. 9 imperfectly understood the thrust of the plot of chs. 1–8. He knew chs. 1–8 only superficially as a story of Jewish triumph over a heathen plot—which indeed it is—and lacked the subtlety to imagine a victory that could not be quantified by a body-count (1984:40).

The text beginning in chapter 9 "strikes out in new directions which have not been prepared for and sometimes run counter to the plot of chs. 1–8" (1984:29). Compared to chapters 1–8, chapters 9–10 are characterized by "distinctly inferior narrative artistry" (1984:30). One finds evidence of the "skill of the author" in the core of the Masoretic story of chapters 1–8, but "literary and narrative weaknesses" in chapters 9–10 (1984:30).[12] Clines is certainly correct that the narrator presents a massacre of anti-Semites rather than a battle of self-defense (8:11) against an imperially sponsored pogrom. But do we have sufficient reason for separating chapters 9 and 10 from chapters 1–8, and "thus for severing the Purim connection altogether" (1984:50)?

This initiative and attack is surprising, and what we read in chapter 9 is "more than" the self-defense we were expecting (8:11). However, if our claim is legitimate that the book of Esther anticipates the genre of turnabout and mock crownings and decrownings, then the final scenes may legitimately be read as something other than appendices to the story proper. My point is that *one reads the final chapters, and indeed the entire book, quite differently if viewing the plot through the lens of the literary carnivalesque.* Indeed, if this narrative world has been carnivalized, these often perceived incongruities may actually be integral parts of the story.

Our understanding of genre influences our interpretation, and if chapters 8 and 9 of Esther are part of the antique literary carnivalesque tradition, it is necessary to situate the moral/ethical question—On what grounds can the staged massacres of 75,810[13] people be justified?—squarely within the realm of the carnivalesque itself. What type of war is this? And how are we to view these massacres?

While it is true that the narrator provides a specific report of casualties in 9:6, 7-10, 15, and 16, much is left unsaid. Where in the citadel does the fighting take place? Do the 500 victims in Susa resist? *How* do the attackers, a "people scattered and separated among the peoples in all the provinces" (3:8), escape harm? These are questions that do not concern our author. Haman's sons are mentioned by name (9:7-9), but do they deserve to be executed for Haman's crime? The author gives no clue that they conspire with him. One way to answer the question is to notice that their execution completes Haman's downfall. The sons are the descendants of Amalek, and the extermination of Haman's house "blots out the memory of Amalek," as the Deuteronomistic Historian had projected (Deut 25:19). But since this is the world of turnabout, 5:11 provides us with an important clue. Here the narrator reports that Haman boasts before his friends and wife about "the splendor of his riches, the number of his sons, all the promotions with which the king had honored him," and so forth. The subsequent execution of Haman's sons, *as projected in this narrative world*, is a turnabout image. Haman is not proud of his sons, but of the number of his sons, and the death of all ten in chapter 9 is a literary attack on the (dead) man's pride. Indeed, chapter 9 also reveals the ultimate reversal: a minority threatened with annihilation because of one man, kills 75,810 without experiencing a single casualty!

Throughout this discussion of the final chapters of Esther, I have hinted that this story about Jewish survival in the diaspora is a unified literary composition by offering a few reasons why the book may not have the "literary flaws" that commentators sometimes find. In sum, this war is a "literary" war.[14] In addition to Haman's sons who are featured in the turnabout image mentioned above, one also notices that the forecasted massacre of women and children in 8:11 parallels 3:13. In chapters 1–7, the "city" of Susa (4:1, 6; 6:9, 11) is distinct from the "citadel" of Susa (1:2, 5; 2:3, 5, 8; 3:15), and this distinction is also maintained at the end of the book. The Jews kill 500 enemies in the citadel (9:6), and then 300 in the city (9:15). The writer here portrays "overkill." More than 75,000 non-Jews are killed without any injury whatsoever to any Jewish partisan, and these victims are spread throughout the kingdom. There is absolutely no mention of pain or blood—only reports of unrealistic casualty figures. Is it possible to execute such a large number without suffering a single casualty? The figure represents such an exaggerated casualty that the Esther (B) translator reduces the number to 15,000! The report indicates effortless victories, but exaggeration or hyperbole certainly does not begin in chapter 9. One has only to think of the earlier images: a party that lasts 180 days, "all" beautiful virgins from throughout the 127 provinces from India to Ethiopia who are brought to the citadel of Susa, one-year cosmetic treatments that are given to thousands of women, royal edicts that are sent "to all the royal provinces, to every province in its own script, and to every people in its own language" (1:22; cf. 3:12-15; 8:9-14). Overkill *follows* overstatement. This is a carnivalesque war!

THE CARNIVALESQUE AND THE FOOL

Low folkloric forms of satire and parody developed simultaneously with high forms of literature in the late Middle Ages. With roots in both classical antiquity and the ancient Orient, this folk literature proved enormously significant for the development of the European novel (Bakhtin 1981:158). While discussing the low folkloric forms of satire and parody, Bakhtin calls attention to carnival's deliberate degradation of rank and authority by means of opposition: "Carnival brings together, unites, weds, and combines the sacred with the profane, the lofty with the lowly, the great with the insignificant, the wise with the stupid."[15] The characters who appear on the pages of carnivalesque writings are sometimes coarse, dirty, and rampantly physical; but it is Bakhtin's concern with "the wise" and "the stupid" that concerns us in this section.

The figures that appear in the folkloric or semi-folkloric forms of satire and parody are the rogue, clown, and fool. It is these three figures who are "the constant, accredited representatives of the carnival spirit in everyday life out of carnival season" (1984b:8). The rogue, unlike the clown and the fool, has some ties that bind him or her to "real life." The clown and the fool, on the other hand, are not of "this world." They possess their unique "rights and privileges" (1981:159). Bakhtin contends that the clown and fool represent a unique form of life, one that is both real and ideal simultaneously. They exist in their own "chronotope," in a realm between life and art.[16] The clown and fool neither fully participate, nor do they understand the conventions which are being exposed, and it is this device of not understanding that exposes conventionality in all its flaws.

Bakhtin comments on the function of the rogue, clown, and fool in the low folkloric forms of medieval literature that tend toward political satire and parody in *The Dialogic Imagination* (1981:158-67). He alludes to the significance these figures have for the later development of the European novel and contends that these characters, familiar figures from classical antiquity, create a special world around themselves. The clown and fool appear in full view at the public square where the common people congregate. They are connected to the theatrical trappings of the public square, and they wear the mask of public spectacle. While discussing the rogue, clown, and fool, Bakhtin shows his primary interest in the characteristics of medieval folk humor. But he is often interested in issues of historical poetics, and he looks back to classical antiquity where he finds the roots for the these unique literary types. He suggests that it is through the representation of clowns and fools in everyday carnival life that the traditions of carnival and of "commedia dell'arte" continued in one form or another through the centuries to emerge full-blown with Rabelais.

The fool or clown is the king of the upside down world. While in early forms the fool is viewed negatively, by the time of the late Middle Ages, the literary fool has assumed a protean form and is not pure negation. We find justification for linking the story of Esther to the literary carnivalesque once again because in such a system it is the king who is the clown. In the world of turnabout, the king is elected and mocked by all the people. At the end of his reign, he is "abused and beaten . . . just as the carnival dummy of winter or of the dying year is mocked, beaten, torn to pieces, burned, or drowned" (1984b: 197). In the story of Esther, as we will soon discover, King Ahasuerus and his subordinate Haman assume the literary carnivalesque form of the fool together. But if Haman and Ahasuerus are the fools in the story of Esther, they are not the typical fools because the prototype figures of the late Middle Ages are not only laughed at by others but also by themselves:

> These figures are laughed at by others, and *themselves* as well. Their laughter bears the stamp of the public square where the folk gather. They re-establish the public nature of the human figure: the entire being of characters such as these is, after all, utterly on the surface; everything is brought out on to the square, so to speak; their entire function consists in externalizing things (1981:159-60; original emphasis).

These unique characters are important for another reason: they produce parodic laughter. Laughter deflates authority, and Bakhtin cites it as a factor of decisive importance to the novel. He also argues that laughter originally represents language through the "ridiculing of another's language and another's direct discourse" (1981:50). Laughing at another's discourse—especially at authoritative discourse—is a means of debasing authority, of drawing near what had been far away, of getting close to what had previously been private, or of unmasking what had been veiled and what had functioned as an oppressive veil. Hence laughter and its accompanying travesty forms "prepared the ground for the novel" by liberating the object of discourse from the net of authoritative language and by destroying "the homogenizing power of myth over language." In this way, laughter "freed consciousness from the power of the direct word, destroyed the thick walls that had imprisoned consciousness within its own discourse" (1981:60). Thus, Bakhtin's main point is that laughter made language its own object of representation. Once the direct word—especially the word that would have the last word—was robbed of its power, the dialogical word was free to pursue a liberating act by means of laughter.

By the time the literary carnivalesque is full-blown, the rogue, clown, and fool make sport of old authority, but in the story of Esther fools often occupy positions of authority. Bakhtin's ideas about old authority and truth masquerading as absolutes have implications when we consider the fools in our story:

> They cannot and do not wish to laugh; they strut majestically, consider their foes the enemies of eternal truth, and threaten them with eternal punishment. They do not see themselves in the mirror of time, do not perceive their own origin, limitations and end; they do not recognize their own ridiculous faces or the comic nature of their pretentions to eternity and immutability. And thus these personages come to the end of their role still serious, although their spectators have been laughing for a long time (1984b:212).

What are the effects of representing persons in a ridiculous, carnivalesque way in the Esther story? And what is the effect of the parodic laughter they engender?

ESTHER AND THE FOOL(S)

The observation that literary fools occupy center stage in the book of Esther is not new,[17] but it appears that this character type has not been viewed in the light of the literary carnivalesque before. Both Ahasuerus and Haman are portrayed as "fools" in this story, and their folly is highlighted—to mention just one example—when the king and vizier sit down for drinks as the capital city is thrown into confusion. But the foolishness of Haman and Ahasuerus is represented in crucially different ways in this scene and throughout the story. For his part, Haman celebrates because the king has just given him *carte blanche* permission to do with the Jews as he wishes. The king, on the other hand, has turned the whole matter into yet another occasion for indulgence. Let us consider how these two fools are portrayed.

Ahasuerus

Throughout, Ahasuerus is portrayed as all surface. His desire for an ostentatious display of wealth is introduced in the opening scene and reinforced at almost every turn. Ahasuerus attempts to buy the admiration of others, and those who arrive at his marathon banquets experience his generosity first hand. They also have a chance to see how the king displays his wealth. When Esther is crowned, he grants "amnesty"[18] and "gives gifts with royal liberality" (2:18). The king is also given to grandstanding. When Haman appeals to the king to issue a decree calling for the destruction of "a certain people" (3:8), he offers to place "ten thousand talents of silver" into the royal treasury, but the king will have none of it: "Keep the money and do with the people as you please," he tells Haman (3:11). In the scenes that follow, the king three times offers Esther half the kingdom (5:3, 6; 7:2), and, after learning that the Jews killed five hundred Susans as well as the ten sons of Haman, the king asks the queen what more he can grant. He reassures her that "it shall be fulfilled" (9:12).

The narrator sometimes exposes Ahasuerus's mind. These inside views expose Ahasuerus as a simple, foolhardy man. He is too often, it seems, "pleased," that is, satisfied. The advice that Memucan offers at the end of chapter 1 "pleases the king" (v. 21) as does the advice the king's servants give at 2:4. Esther also "pleases him" and "wins his favor." Ahasuerus "loves" and "favors" Esther more than all the other women precisely because she "pleases" him the most (2:9, 14, 17). On other occasions the king's anger is exposed, but it quickly and superficially subsides. When Queen Vashti refuses to come at Ahasuerus's bidding, he becomes "enraged, and his anger burned within him," but, after learning from Memucan how to save face, the narrator reports that "the anger of King Ahasuerus abated" (2:1). Later, when Esther reveals to the king that Haman has plotted against her people, the narrator again reports that the king rises from the feast "in wrath" only to report three verses later that "the anger of the king abated" after Harbona suggested a way to resolve the crisis (7:7, 10).

The intense emotions that Ahasuerus frequently experiences (rage, anger, pleasure) contrast with the thoughts he apparently so seldom has. He first permits the destruction of many of his subjects and then must allow thousands of people to be destroyed to save the original intended victims. It is "hard to imagine," Michael Fox observes, "[Ahasuerus] having any thoughts not obvious to anyone. . . . His most dangerous flaw is his failure to think" (1991:171). This *tabula rasa* is disturbing because the king transfers the thinking ("Do whatever seems good to you" [3:11]) to a man who does have the mental capacity to contrive an inane plan of truly epic proportions. Ahasuerus often *needs* advice. The narrator informs us of his routine practice of seeking advice from others early in this story by reporting that "this was the king's procedure" (1:13), and when he receives directions from others, he fails to ask for details. When Haman enlists the king's support to destroy "a certain people," Ahasuerus does not even bother to ask which people are being disposed. When the king arrives at both banquets that Esther prepares for him, his words reflect his blithe manner. He appears anxious to grant whatever petition she might have— notice the repetition in his quoted speech and his desire to have Haman brought "quickly" so that Esther may have her wish (5:3-6)—but evinces no curiosity when she postpones her response until yet another banquet (5:3-8). He demonstrates another cavalier, non-reflective attitude in chapter 6 when he unintentionally humiliates Haman by elevating Mordecai to the prominent position of sitting on the king's horse and riding through the open square of the city. How can Ahasuerus *not* know that Haman would love to wear the royal robes and royal crown and ride on the royal horse's back? In only one instance does Ahasuerus refuse the advice or petition that is made of him, but even at this point—when he indicates that he cannot rescind his own decree in 8:7-8—he grants Mordecai and Esther authority to write as they wish with the king's ring (8:8).

Ahasuerus twice cavalierly transfers extraordinary authority to others (3:10; 8:8). In the first instance, Haman constructs a scenario of far-reaching danger through a series of arguments while appealing to the king's interests. In the process he apparently relies on Ahasuerus's laziness when asking for the pogrom. Note how Haman does the king's thinking for him: "If it pleases the king, let a decree be issued for their destruction" (3:9). "Let a decree be issued," Haman asks, without naming a decree-writer. Let someone (else) write it, Haman proposes. I'll work out the details. And the king hears Haman. "So the king took his signet ring from his hand and gave it to Haman," to do with as he pleased (3:10-11). And maybe it's just as well that the king leaves the details to someone else when it comes to decree writing. When he earlier issued a command that each man in the kingdom should have dominion in his own house, the narrator hints that he alters Memucan's advice. Memucan had advised the king to oust Vashti and replace her so that women might learn to honor their husbands from this example (1:19-20), but the king's letter declares that "every man should be master in his own house" (1:22). The irony of Ahasuerus's imperial edict is that by legislating "that every man should be master in his own house" (that is, that every wife should obey her husband), the king writes into law what he has been unable to do himself.

The suggestions Ahasuerus receives in the opening chapters anticipate future events. In a transition scene at the beginning of chapter 2, the narrator reports that Ahasuerus remembered Vashti and what she had done (v. 1). The word "remember" is seldom applied to Ahasuerus, and in this instance, the final clause of the king's remembering is rendered as a passive construction, "what had been decreed against her." The verbal tense functions to remind us that the action taken against Vashti was not Ahasuerus's independent decision (Fox 1991:26). Of course, the servants suggest a let-the-most-beautiful-virgin-be-found plan to Ahasuerus. He likes what he hears. It "pleased the king, and he did so" (2:4).

In chapter 7, when the king misinterprets Haman's pleading

with Esther as a sexual advance, the king is advised what to do. Harbona, one of the king's eunuchs, transforms Ahasuerus's question, "Will [Haman] even assault the queen in my presence, in my own house?" (v. 8), into an occasion for rendering advice. The eunuch promptly suggests a way to resolve the crisis by pointing out that a solution is near at hand: "Look, the very gallows that Haman has prepared for Mordecai . . . stands at Haman's house" (v. 9). In his confused fury, the king takes Harbona's cue and resolves the whole affair with only a few words, "Hang him on that" (v. 9). The Jews are spared precisely because of Ahasuerus *misperception*: Haman is hanged not because he tried to kill all the Jews but because the king thought he was assaulting the queen!

The narrator also provides a few clues to suggest the king is short on memory. The action taken against the would-be assassins is recorded in the book of the annals, and even though this writing is done "in the presence of the king" (2:23), Ahasuerus gives it no thought until the night when he cannot sleep. He orders that the annals be read to him, and the reminder that Mordecai saved the king's life prompts him to ask, "What honor or distinction has been bestowed on Mordecai for this?" (6:3a). The king's questions that follow in this scene also suggest his lack of perception: "Who is in the court?" (6:4), and "What shall be done for the man whom the king wishes to honor?" (6:6). Clueless, Ahasuerus seeks advice.

The king's short memory is highlighted on another occasion. When Esther reveals to the king that she and her people have been sold, "to be destroyed, to be killed, and to be annihilated," the king asks, "Who is he, and where is he, who has presumed to do this?" (7:5). It is true that the king had not bothered to find out which people would suffer in the forecasted pogrom back in chapter 3, but now in chapter 7, even with Haman in his presence, the king forgets that he had given his vizier permission to do as he pleased with "a certain people."

Call it laziness or stupidity, this king tends to let people do whatever they want. The result of Ahasuerus's indolence is that others seize the opportunity to think for him, and in the process they often exact their own wills. His problems are compounded by the evil intentions and bad advice from those who are near him. The king has surrounded himself with buffoons on all sides. When Vashti defies his authority by refusing to be displayed before the people, Ahasuerus allows himself to be manipulated, to be convinced that it's in his best interest to banish his beautiful—a trait Ahasuerus no doubt admires—wife. The counsel that Memucan gives is certainly poor advice: "Not only has Queen Vashti done wrong to the king, but also to all the officials and all the peoples who are in all the provinces of King Ahasuerus. For this deed of the queen will be made known to all women." Memucan's words reflect more the feelings of those at the palace than upon "all women" throughout "all the provinces." Michael Fox refers to the "paper patriarchs" at the palace and concludes that "they, like the king, are desperate for honor, and they think they can achieve it by decree" (1991:24). Without any thought about the absurdity, enforceability, or cost of such a ludicrous decree, the narrator reports, quite simply, that the king liked the advice and did as Memucan proposed (1:21).

Ahasuerus's dim wits and short memory have a dramatic effect on the plot. Indeed, much of the story proceeds because Ahasuerus functions as a literary fool. The solicited and unsolicited advice and petitions of Memucan, the servants, Haman, Harbona, Esther, and Mordecai serve collectively to move the plot forward. Ahasuerus, the fool, is a dangerous man, not because he is inherently vicious or even anti-Jewish, but because in the land of Persia he has absolute power. His indifference is dangerous because he so willingly hands power over to another fool, a man with insidious plans of his own.

Haman

If Ahasuerus is a dolt, Haman is certainly a conniving dolt, a clever fool. Haman falls in this story, not because he lacks wit, but because of his distended pride. He is often running about. He hurries to the banquet, hurries to parade Mordecai through the streets, and then hurries home in grief (5:5; 6:10, 12; Fox 1991:80). A crafty buffoon who knows nothing about self-control, he is sometimes thought to personify Wisdom's concept of a fool, a person who boasts of his or her riches and good fortune but whose life is based on insecure mooring.[19] Michael Fox has observed, correctly I believe, that Haman's folly is not entirely consistent with the form described in Wisdom literature (1991:182). By the Bible's standards, Haman is a developed character. That is, his characterization is achieved from a number of angles in this story in a way that is more consistent with the fool of the literary carnivalesque tradition than with Wisdom's fool. Unlike Ahasuerus, who desires a big meal and lavish display, the narrator portrays Haman as a man with motives. He plots, he acts, and he carries out his hidden agenda. Moreover, he's loquacious—too often disclosing his thoughts to others (5:12-13). His rage makes him imprudent (3:5-6), and he is a conceited man who thinks he's the only one worthy of receiving the king's honor (6:6).

The characterization of Haman is accomplished through reports of his action and speech, that is, through external views visible to characters in the narrative world and to the audience as well. The narrator also describes Haman's inner life, his emotions and thoughts. Since external views are available to all, portrayal by means of the inner life represents a special case because the information conveyed is privileged. We are not told precisely what motivates Mordecai to refuse to bow, but we are told how Mordecai's non-compliance makes Haman feel. Just as Ahasuerus needed his power validated by Vashti, Haman needs his validated by Mordecai. Haman holds a high position in the land, but within he craves something else. Power is not enough for him: he needs absolute power, absolute control, absolute domination. When Mordecai refuses to bow, Haman becomes a very unhappy man, but, in this narrative world of the turnabout, Haman's mood will change. After banqueting with the king and queen, Haman leaves the palace bursting with pride—only to become infuriated when he sees Mordecai (5:9).

Such attention to Haman's inner life is not new. Ahasuerus's emotional state, we noted, was also revealed. But as we view Haman's mind at work, we discover that he is a *thinker*. Just after the narrator reports that he "thought it beneath him to lay hands on Mordecai alone" (3:6), Haman, the fool, garners the king's good wishes as he plots to destroy a people. In chapter 3

Haman is portrayed as a shrewd and evil man, and from this point on he will be exposed as a man driven by his impulses and hatred for Mordecai. Even though a law authorizing the massacre of Mordecai and his people has been written, Haman is unable to wait for the day of destruction. His desire for revenge drives him to build the gallows that will be used to bring about his own humiliation and death.

Haman makes a fool of himself when revealing his assumption that he alone is worthy of the king's honor in chapter 6. We view the fool as the narrator reveals his inner thoughts: "Haman said to himself, 'Whom would the king wish to honor more than me?'" (v. 6). Describing the ceremony in which he hopes to be honored, he does not mention money or a high political office (vv. 7-9). These he has. Haman has an insatiable appetite for recognition, as we discovered from his response to Mordecai in chapter 3, and he wants *more* of it now.

In contrast to this story's fools, Esther and Mordecai emerge as exemplary literary opposites: they are rational, sensible, and courageous. They knew when to speak and when to sit silent. For her part, Esther is portrayed as a contemplative, one who considers her actions' possible consequences before she acts. Both she and Mordecai also have the ability to secure friendships, or at least to win the confidence and respect of those whom they meet at court. Hegai is not only a eunuch who has "custody" of Esther. He treats her as a friend and assists her to the "best place in the harem" (2:9). Hathach and the other servants transfer messages clandestinely and keep secrets for Mordecai and Esther (4:4-11). And finally, at the time of Haman's unmasking, we discover that it is Harbona, another of the king's eunuchs, who suggests the means of Haman's punishment (7:9).

In sum, we discover in art, as we do in life, that fools sometimes end up in high positions with power. The commentary on fools in the Esther story is expressed by the prince in *Amadeus* who, when pressed to explain the faults he finds in Mozart's music, can only say, "Too many notes."

6

PURIM

THE CARNIVALESQUE AND COLLECTIVE GAIETY

The carnival spirit with its freedom, its utopian character oriented toward the future, was gradually transformed into a mere holiday mood.
—Mikhail Bakhtin, *Rabelais and His World*

I know of no other way of coping with great tasks, than play.
—Friedrich Nietzsche, quoted by Monford Harris,
"Purim: The Celebration of Dis-Order"

Then Mordecai went out from the presence of the king, wearing royal robes of blue and white, with a great golden crown and a mantle of fine linen and purple, while the city of Susa shouted and rejoiced. For the Jews there was light and gladness, joy and honor. In every province and in every city, wherever the king's command and his edict came, there was gladness and joy among the Jews, a festival and a holiday.
—Esth 8:15-17a

. . . making that a day of feasting and gladness. Therefore the Jews of the villages, who live in the open towns, hold the fourteenth day of the month of Adar as a day for gladness and feasting, a holiday on which they send gifts of food to one another.
—Esth 9:18b-19

The Hebrew version of the Esther story ends with a strong element of play. Our attention is drawn throughout to the grave danger that Esther and Mordecai seek to overcome, and only after a series of reversals does the story conclude with a note of festive joy. Everyone opposed to the wicked Haman and Ahasuerus gains a chance for celebration. We find words such as "gladness," "joy," "festival," "holiday," and "feasting" appearing once or twice at the end of the tale, and this gaiety reflects a mood that is different from the pompous display of wealth in the opening chapters. What are we to make of this rejoicing? Why this celebratory mood? And what is laughter and celebration doing in a book where all the Jews throughout the Persian empire are almost destroyed and where the enemies of the Jews are destroyed (8:13; 9:5)?

The author is emphasizing collective gaiety in the final chapters, but we should remember that both the misogyny and the planned pogroms that occupy much narrative space in the Esther tale are terrifyingly real. Michael Fox's astute observation about the book's strange humor provides a working context for the discussion that follows:

> The book's incongruous humor is one of its strange hallmarks. It mixes laughter with fear in telling about a near-tragedy that is chillingly reminiscent of actual tragedies. We laugh at the confused sexual politicians, the quirky emperor, and, above all, the ludicrous, self-glorifying, self-destructive villain. This is almost literally gallows humor, except that the gallows are finally used on the hangman. Humor, especially the humor of ridicule, is a device for defusing fear. The author teaches us to make fun of the very forces that once threatened—and will again threaten—our existence, and thereby makes us recognize their triviality as well as their power. "If I laugh at any mortal thing," said Byron, "t'is that I may not weep" (1991:253).

Bakhtin himself also provides a context for understanding this unique laughter. The laughter he envisions *does* something. It brings something crude close up so that we can examine it. He writes:

> It is precisely laughter that destroys . . . any hierarchical (distancing and valorized) distance. As a distanced image a subject cannot be comical; to be made comical, it must be brought close. Everything that makes us laugh is close at hand, all comical creativity works in a zone of maximal proximity. Laughter has the remarkable power of making an object come up close, of drawing it into a zone of crude contact where one can finger it familiarly on all sides, turn it upside down, inside out, peer at it from above and below, break

open its external shell, look into its center, doubt it, take it apart, dismember it, lay it bare and expose it, examine it freely and experiment with it. Laughter demolishes fear and piety before an object, before a world, making of it an object of familiar contact and thus clearing the ground for an abso- lutely free investigation of it. Laughter is a vital factor in laying down that prerequisite for fearlessness without which it would be impossible to approach the world realistically (1981:23).

Before proceeding, it may be worth remembering that the ending has often been discounted.[1] Maybe a book so preoccu- pied with death should not convey a festive mood at the end? Someone—Does it really matter if it is the author or an edi- tor?—added these verses to the story, and for good reason. My purpose in this chapter is to link the ancient tradition of carnival laughter to the book of Esther while offering a few observations from which the book's terminus may be viewed. We shall return to the story of Esther, but a few questions will be posed first: What is the nature of carnival laughter? How did it develop through history? What is the relationship between carnival laughter in life and art? And in what way is laughter a social phenomenon?

The Uniqueness of Carnival Laughter

Rabelais and His World is a history of carnival laughter or the laughter of people in the marketplace. Such laughter reach- es its high point in the writings of Rabelais, and festive laugh- ter is dominant in all of his sign systems. Laughter, the supreme truth and custodian of human freedom, is the fulcrum of Bakh- tin's entire aesthetics. It alone can unify culture because it is accessible to everyone, and in any literary form where car- nival laughter appears, the gaiety has roots in folk culture it- self.

Bakhtin has a specific type of laughter in mind when he writes about people who gather in the marketplace. He is not concerned with "the individual gaiety of a [child] let loose from a smoky hut but the collective gaiety of the people gathered at the fair, not the naïve gaiety of a [child] 'rushing madly across puddles' but a popular, festive gaiety that was gradually formed during many centuries" (1984b:146). Carnival laughter must not be confused with mere holiday play or state sponsored festivals because its license does not derive from any official calendar, but from a force which exists before the time of priests and kings and to whose superior power they defer when licensing carnival. The force where carnival finds its true origin and sanction is folk laughter, and some parts of the world are accessible only to laughter. In essence, folk laughter removes carnivalized collectives from serious, "proper" life. This kind of laughter eventually reaches a high point in the Renaissance, and the centuries-long tradition of folk humor and accompanying laughter has a deep philosophical meaning which provides a peculiar point of view relative to the world. The collective gaiety of the people at the fair allows us to see the world anew, and perhaps more profoundly than when we see it from the serious standpoint.

The figures associated with carnival laughter—the fool, clown, and rogue—are the very foundation and the most subversive elements in Bakhtin's critique of tradition and ideology. In a sense, laughter is more fundamental and subversive than dialogue, or, more accurately, laughter is the most radical form of dialogue.[2] It is laughter that resists and undermines the power of all authoritarian systems and institutions and thus makes dialogue possible, even within monolithic, totalitarian structures which function to exclude or repress it.[3]

Carnival laughter has three characteristics. It is corporate, universal, and ambivalent. Carnival laughter is first of all not that of an individual reacting to an isolated "comic" event. It is the laughter of the crowd in the marketplace, "the collective gaiety of the people gathered at the fair" (Bakhtin 1984b:146). Folk culture gives depth to the carnivalized images of collectives, and within folk culture we witness the gay demise of officialdom. Festive art entertains, but it also gives voice to the concerns of an entire group, providing a mixture of social critique and compensation fantasy. While the official world enforces restraint, the carnival world produces freedom and fearlessness:

> The individual feels he [or she] is an indissoluble part of the collectivity, a member of the people's mass body. In this whole the individual body ceases to a certain extent to be itself; it is possible, so to say, to exchange bodies, to be renewed (through change of costume and mask). At the same time the people become aware of their sensual, material bodily unity and community (Bakhtin 1984b:255).

Carnival laughter is thus impersonal, directed to the highest ideals of a community rather than to comic events themselves. The laughter of carnival celebration dissolves the distance between the ideal and the real, and the spirit of this laughter must be understood in a public, communal context.

Second, carnival laughter is universal in scope. No one can escape this laughter: "it is directed at all and everyone. . . . The entire world is seen in its droll aspect, in its gay relativity" (Bakhtin 1984b:11). This "profoundly universal laughter" reflects an outlook on the world (Bakhtin 1984a:127). Everyone can laugh at everyone and everything, including the sacred and the official, because in Bakhtin's festive marketplace there is a temporary suspension of all hierarchical rank. The suspension creates a new community where exchanges are between equals and are as frank and free as language itself. The exchanges are often to the point of obscenity and abuse. The physical body is reviled and celebrated. Universal laughter is in the air.

Third, this type of laughter is ambivalent: "it is gay, triumphant, and at the same time mocking, deriding. It asserts and denies, it buries and revives" (Bakhtin 1984b:11-12). Those who laugh are merry and exultant and simultaneously mocking and ridiculing. Such laughter is therefore an *attitude* which answers to the experience of ambivalence while allowing humankind a vehicle by which to overcome paralyzing fear.

> The satirist whose laughter is negative places himself [or herself] above the object of his [or her] mockery, he [or she] is opposed to it. The wholeness of the world's comic aspect is destroyed, and that which appears comic becomes a private reaction. The people's ambivalent laughter, on the other hand, expresses the point of view of the whole world; he [or she] who is laughing also belongs to it (Bakhtin 1984b:12).

Carnival Laughter through History

Bakhtin calls attention to the historical aspect of festivity, its role as an agent of change, its role in focusing with peculiar sharpness and delicacy the fundamental economic, social, and cultural transformations of early ages. He finds that the festivity, celebration, and holiday mood has certain characteristics which are consistently brought out in carnival rituals and parodies throughout history. During the early Middle Ages this folk humor was restricted to feasts and recreations, but by the late fifteenth century, the culture of laughter had begun to break through and enter all spheres of ideological life. Many cultures had their unofficial carnival side, but during the Renaissance the laughter culture came into full view. The sixteenth century represents the high point in the history of carnival laughter, and within this apex Rabelais's novel, *Gargantua and Pantagruel*, is the crowning achievement. Rabelais's art represents "a new free and critical historical consciousness" (Bakhtin 1984b:97). Yet the importance of Rabelais is not simply the unique place he occupies in the history of literature, but the lesson he provides for political and literary history:

> Rabelais' basic goal was to destroy the official picture of events. . . . He summoned all the resources of sober popular imagery in order to break up official lies and the narrow seriousness dictated by the ruling classes. Rabelais did not implicitly believe in what his time "said and imagined about itself"; he strove to disclose its true meaning for the people (Bakhtin 1984b:439).

Rabelais's laughter, which grew out of the soil of folk humor culture, has, however, often been misunderstood. His laughter, unlike that of a satirist, does not mock or deride.[4] Rabelais's laughter elucidates what is fundamental about his creation, but what is important for our study of Esther is that the ancient tradition prepared the way for this supreme form of laughter. When Bakhtin quotes from Pushkin's *Boris Godunov*, a drama in which the folk "has the last word" by laughing at Boris, the usurper of legitimate power, he hopes to establish this laughing folk as an *historical* force: "All the acts of the drama of world history were performed before a chorus of the laughing people.

. . . [However,] not every period of history had Rabelais for coryphaeus" (1984b:474).

In this final passage of *Rabelais and His World*, Bakhtin himself suggests the validity of laughter for epochs before the Renaissance and thus also the broader validity of his own interpretation: "Though [Rabelais] led the popular chorus of only one time, the Renaissance, he so fully and clearly revealed the peculiar and difficult language of the laughing people that his work sheds its light on the folk culture of humor belonging to other ages" (1984b:474). In the main focus of *Rabelais and His World*, Bakhtin assembles an inventory of laughter forms taken from Medieval and Renaissance culture, and he postulates that these forms began in antiquity. The descriptions of "gladness," "joy," "feasting," "a festival," and "a holiday" at the end of the Esther story may indeed be part of this ancient carnival laughter tradition. That is, this early carnival writing appears to find its logical conclusion in the festive mood at the end of the book.[5] Far from being appendices or non-essential elements of the Hebrew tale, the final scenes are what we might expect in this early literary carnivalesque writing.

The Elusive Boundary between Life and Art

For Rabelais and other writers of carnival, society and art merge, and many of Bakhtin's observations on early, middle, and late carnival deal with aesthetic and social situations—on the boundary between life and art. Bakhtin finds that while carnival images closely resemble the artistic forms of the spectacle, they differ in an important way: "but the basic carnival nucleus of this culture is by no means a purely artistic form nor a spectacle and does not, generally speaking, belong to the sphere of art. It belongs to the borderline between art and life. In reality, it is life itself, but shaped according to a certain pattern of play" (1984b:7). From this perspective, a text cannot be grasped through linguistics alone. Bakhtin thus postulates the necessity for what may be called a translinguistic science of inter- and trans-textual relationships. A novel such as *Gargantua and Pantagruel* (or any writing that contains carnivalistic elements) testifies to an enduring need to celebrate, and it also shows us how closely that impulse is bound up with literature, with desires that influence artistic creation and consumption. Bakhtin's book on Rabelais is a celebration of the folk and their hope for the future, and carnival presents the victory of the future over the past. The birth of the new is as indispensable and inevitable as the death of the old. In such works, "the carnivalistic tradition is reborn in a new way: it takes on its own meaning, combines with other artistic elements, furthers its own particular artistic goals" (1984a:159).

Bakhtin thus makes it clear that his research is not merely a scholarly exercise in poetics. He shows that when an official dominating culture loses touch with the people, the folk bring their laughter back into the work of politics: "All the acts of the drama of world history were performed before a chorus of the laughing people. . . . Every act of world history was accompanied by a laughing chorus" (1984b:474). In the opening chapter we observed that while Bakhtin was concerned with form, he is not a Formalist in the strict sense. In fact, he cannot easily be placed in any one literary category. This idea is reinforced when we consider a passage about the boundary between life and art from *Problems of Dostoevsky's Poetics* (emphasis added):

> *Carnival itself* (we repeat: in the sense of a sum total of all diverse festivities of the carnival type) *is not, of course, a literary phenomenon.* It is syncretic pageantry of a ritualistic sort. As a form it is very complex and varied, giving rise, on a general carnivalistic base, to diverse variants and nuances depending upon the epoch, the people, the individual festivity. Carnival has worked out an entire language of symbolic concretely sensuous forms—from large and complex mass actions to individual carnivalistic gestures. This language, in a differentiated and even (as in any language) articulate way, gave expression to a unified (but complex) carnival sense of the world, permeating all its forms. This language cannot be translated in any full or adequate way into a verbal language, and much less into a language of abstract concepts, but it is amenable to a certain transposition into a language of artistic images that has something in common with its concretely sensuous nature; that is, it can be transposed into the language of literature. We are calling this transposition of carnival into the language of literature the carnivalization of literature (1984a:122).[6]

Bakhtin has memorably demonstrated that it is possible to draw an analogy between the role of the carnivalesque in literary works and culture. Whether rhetorical or actual, the carnivalesque occasion, like the masquerade, is always provocative: it intimates an alternative view of the "nature of things" and embodies a liberated escape from the status quo.

Laughter as a Social Phenomenon

Bakhtin is concerned with how laughter functions symbolically and thematically within individual works to make up a writer's distinct social and festive vision, and he eventually conceives of society as an enormous living being, a "great generic body" (1984b:88). Laughter seemingly protects the organism from the harmful effects of authoritarian regimes by realizing what he calls the "material bodily principle." In medieval and early modern Europe, laughter was in the first place a mode of social expression and organization, a point which Bakhtin returns to in his book on Rabelais. Laughter in literature is more than a symbol or part of an overarching structure. As all of Bakhtin's work testifies, his concern with texts was centered not on their internal grammar—again in this sense he is not a Formalist—but on their relationship to society and on their cultural function.

In the laughter of Renaissance folk culture, Bakhtin seized the possibility of a "complete exit from the present order of this life" (1984b:275), and collective gaiety becomes a medium through which communal needs and problems are expressed and fulfilled. Bakhtin reaches this conclusion by recognizing that carnival attitudes depend upon a peculiar consciousness of human community whereby the world becomes meaningful only in dialogue. Meaning does not reside in the head of an individual; it is born in dialogical intercourse *among* people in the marketplace. Carnival blurs the boundaries that normally exist between orders of discourse and between classes. It abolishes the distinction between observer and participant, between satire and the object of satire. There are no footlights in carnival. Participants are simultaneously actors and audience, and all is dissolved in collective gaiety.

But perhaps laughter's most important function as a social

force lies in its ability to deflate and overcome authority. Laughing at another's discourse is a means of deflating authority, of drawing near what had been distant, of unmasking what had functioned as a veil. The carnival world is permeated with collective gaiety that destroys every form of authority, and communal laughter is fundamentally opposed to all hierarchies. This laughter is a subversive force, one which liberates victims from the restrictions of a prevailing order. Celebrating in this context becomes a way of celebrating in time, a way to perceive the transience of existence, and a way to topple the structures of an official society which tries to assert its laws. (One might think of the "irreversible law" which is overcome in the story of Esther.) Popular-festive forms also look to the future. They present the victory of a future golden age over the past. This new age is a time of "victory of all the people's material abundance [and] freedom" (1984b:256). (The festive mood reflected in the Esther tale and transformed into a holiday for all time might also come to mind.)[7]

COLLECTIVE GAIETY
AND ESTHER (M) THROUGH THE AGES

In Bakhtin's Rabelais, even more than in his beloved Aristophanes, grammar becomes laughter in action. The presence of laughter indicates that dialogic interaction is still possible even in the most repressive situations. Only where laughter reigns, can the barriers of apartness that separate human speakers be breached. Laughter's presence also implies that sociability and community survive even at those moments when community is most threatened. There is no standpoint of seriousness counterposed to laughter. Laughter is the only positive force.

Bakhtin's approach to Rabelais, unlike that of previous Rabelais scholars, was to show that this writer's work stems from traditions of popular "laughter culture," and Bakhtin examined in detail how various forms of popular, unofficial art are reflected in Rabelais's work. Carnival itself is not, of course, a literary phenomenon, and collective gaiety is more than part of an overarching structure. But does Bakhtin's attitude towards the Renaissance culture of laughter and towards its literary representatives have any impact on the Hebrew story of Esther's claim to uniqueness? This version of the Esther tale is often described as "the most secular" in the Bible: the book makes no reference to God, prayers, or sacrifices, and the drinking scenes border on debauchery. But perhaps this "anomaly" provides a clue for interpretation. The collective gaiety that emerges in such a pronounced fashion in the final chapters of Esther appears to provide the best justification for linking the story to the culture of laughter and its literary counterpart, the carnivalesque. Issues related to this laughter may best be posed by exploring the accompanying culture of folk humor.

Five books of the Hebrew Bible are known as *megillot* or "scrolls," and they are read on five holidays.[8] The Song of Songs is read on Pesach (Passover), the book of Ruth on Shavuot (Pentecost), Lamentations on Tishoh B'Ov (the Ninth of Ab), Ecclesiastes on Sukkot (the Feast of Booths), and the book of Esther on Purim. The subject matter of the Song of Songs, Ruth, and Ecclesiastes has no real relation to the festivals on which they are read, and Lamentations is only indirectly related to the destruction of the temple. Only the book of Esther is closely associated with the holiday, and one can easily argue that Purim could not be understood without the book of Esther. As Carey Moore notes, "after all, the raison d'être of the Hebrew version was the establishment of Purim" (1977:160). The laughter and celebration which we discover at the end of the story is in response to life in exile.[9] Purim is the only festival that Judaism has that deals explicitly with exile, and this collective gaiety is an annual holiday whereby participants grasp this experience existentially. The other holidays may refer indirectly to exile, but they are clearly not concerned with it (Harris 1977:167).

The Hebrew version of the Esther tale has been understood as part and parcel of laughter culture through the ages, and the dramatization of Purim events began long ago, possibly before the Christian era. The Purim festival had already been established by the second century C.E. when a tractate of the Mishnah was written outlining the details of its observance, and Italian carnival elements were injected during later centuries

(Rylaarsdam:969). Purim stresses the comic; Purim stresses play. Fasts are serious and have no part at the end of the book. After dealing with the subjects of atrocity and domination, we end with Purim and a festive mood. The process leads to a cathartic and rejuvenating return to everyday life.

The collective gaiety is marked by radical differences from everyday life, and excessive behavior affirms life in the midst of a ritual encounter with death. For example, eating and drinking figure prominently in this gay and noisy feast. The Talmud asks celebrants to mellow themselves with drinks on Purim until they can no longer distinguish between "Cursed be Haman" and "Blessed be Mordecai." During the festal meal, mourning is forbidden and the eating lasts into the night of 14 Adar. But eating and drinking are not the only carnival elements that have played a part in Purim celebrations. Other forms of Purim rituals have evolved during a period of two millennia. These forms include the following: mummeries or masquerades, the election of a "Purim king," the hanging of Haman or the burning effigy, Purim plays (also called Purim-shpil), and the rattling of hand held noisemakers.[10]

In Esth 8:15 Mordecai is described as departing from the king "wearing royal robes of blue and white, with a great golden crown and a mantle of fine linen and purple." Mordecai had previously been robed in the royal garb in chapter 6. A tradition developed, perhaps under the influence of these scenes and the influence of Italian carnival (Jacobs 1971:1395), whereby people dress in costumes and masks on Purim. Indeed, Purim eventually became a masquerade festival. This custom reflects a communally controlled transgression whereby ordinary identity and rules of behavior are temporally set aside. During carnival time individuals sacrifice their identities to participate corporately. Sometimes celebrants dress like Esther or Mordecai wearing clothes of a queen and a king. One may even dress as Haman, or in clothes of the opposite sex. By changing clothes, Jews become Gentiles, women become men, and men become women. Roles are reversed. Jewish children also participate in this celebration by donning colorful clothes and by painting their faces. They go from house to house while dancing, singing, and celebrating. These masquerade rituals, a hallmark of carnival, are known as mummeries and began perhaps in the early sixteenth century. Theodor Gaster provides the following description:

> [Mummeries] are today an integral part of [Purim] festivities, and in [Israel], more particularly, there has been a marked revival of them in recent years. The mummeries take the form of what is elsewhere known as "guising." Groups of boys and girls, grotesquely robed, masked, and bedaubed in the most garish and outlandish of colors, make the rounds of Jewish homes, somewhat in the manner of carol singers, chanting doggerel verses in Yiddish and soliciting small monetary rewards (1950:59).

The election of a king, another key symbolic gesture of carnival, also became part of Purim celebrations. One month before the festival is inaugurated, the Purim king is solemnly crowned during a mock coronation scene. In this spirit of masquerade, a child might also be elected "Purim-king" and given some authority during the celebration. These customs originated in the Middle Ages in Provence.

Another Purim custom that developed is that of burning or hanging Haman in effigy. The custom is at least as old as the fifth century and was especially popular during the ninth and tenth centuries. A pole is erected in a courtyard, and the Haman effigy is hung on it. The effigy is then doused with a flammable liquid and ignited while the celebrants stand around clapping, singing, and rejoicing. This custom is still observed in Iran and Kurdistan, and it is also part of the modern day Purim celebration in Tel Aviv.

The custom of Purim plays (or Purim-shpil) also developed alongside the mummery, election, and effigy traditions. In a light, frivolous monologue a performer will sometimes appear in costume and recite rhymed paraphrases from the story of Esther as well as parodies on liturgical texts in an effort to entertain the audience. Early forms of Purim plays can be dated to the second half of the sixteenth century. These monologues eventually became more complex and dramatic in form. They also became more parodic and humorous. The Purim plays were most often presented in private homes during the festive family meal, and in addition to costumes, the performers wore masks. The obscenities of Renaissance carnival, which Bakhtin frequently alludes to, cannot be linked to the Esther narrative itself, but this emphasis on what Bakhtin calls the "lower bodily stratum" did develop in time. According to Theodor Gaster (1950:68-69), frivolity eventually became of "so coarse a nature" that some Jewish authorities ordered that the performances be stopped. And Chone Shmeruk, writing about the Purim plays, notes that "profanity and obscenity of an erotic nature" became elements of the humorous play (1971:1402).

The celebration of Purim is also marked by carefully orchestrated noise. The one who reads the scroll pronounces the four verses of redemption (2:5; 8:15, 16; and 10:3) with a louder voice than when reading the other verses. Loud noises are made with hand held noisemakers whenever Haman's name is read from the scroll in order to blot out the memory of Amalek (Esth 3:1; cf. 1 Sam 15:8-9). Schauss (1938:258) even alludes to fireworks which are used instead of rattles in some celebrations.

COLLECTIVE GAIETY
AND ESTHER (M) AT ITS INCEPTION

Festivals, originating as folk customs, are subsequently shaped by cultural factors, and it is often assumed that Christian carnival influenced Purim festivals during the Middle Ages, especially in Italy. It is, therefore, not difficult to show that the story of Esther is related to carnival customs as they developed through the centuries. But can it be demonstrated that the Esther story *at its inception* was associated with early forms of carnival? On what grounds might we argue that the masquerade, the noise-making, and so forth belong to a carnival concept of the world from the very start? Is there a link between the literary and early social carnivalesque?

This study of the story has suggested that the text shows affinities with carnival life, and the Purim festivals at the end of the narrative provide yet another example of the story's carnivalesque cast. The author describes the celebration at the end of the story as an enduring festival and holiday:

In every province and in every city . . . there was gladness
and joy among the Jews, a festival and a holiday (8:17).

Therefore the Jews of the villages . . . hold the fourteenth day
of the month of Adar as a day for gladness and feasting, a
holiday (9:19).

They should keep the fourteenth day of the month Adar and
also the fifteenth day of the same month, year by year . . . as
the month that had been turned for them from sorrow into
gladness and from mourning into a holiday (9:21-22).

These days should be remembered and kept throughout every
generation, in every family, province, and city; and these days
of Purim should never fall into disuse among the Jews, nor
should the commemoration of these days cease among their
descendants (9:28).

Holidays are for everyone in the community, and this gay
celebration is corporate in nature. The victory does not belong
to Esther or Mordecai; all intended victims triumph. And the
rejoicing at the end of the tale is widespread: "these days
should be remembered and kept throughout every generation,
in every family, province, and city" (9:28). This holiday rejuve-
nates society by creating the world anew, and it endures. The
Talmud proclaims that Purim would remain even if all other holidays would disappear (Fredman 1976:111; Harris 1977:170).

Bakhtin identifies the festive literary genre with "the very
core of the carnival sense of the world—the pathos of shifts and
changes, of death and renewal. Carnival is the festival of
all-annihilating and all-renewing time" (1984a:124). Festivals
celebrate violation of rules and decorum as well as the return of
the everyday world. When Bakhtin writes of a festive vision he
means life viewed in terms of celebration. The impulse to
celebrate helps define and create community, and the celebration itself allows individuals to come to grips with mortality. He
argues that such visions are older than the Christian era and
that they once played an indisputably central role in life. Never-
theless, carnival is not simply recreation: "Carnival is the people's second life, organized on the basis of laughter. It is a
festive life. Festivity is a peculiar quality of all comic rituals and
spectacles" (1984b:8). At its inception, Purim celebrates the

conflict between order and chaos, stability and change, and the holiday gains its character from the struggle between authority and license.

A Seasonal Festival

It is worth remembering that all reconstructions of the earliest Purim celebrations require speculation. We rely upon conjecture. By the fifteenth century, Purim celebrations had acquired new forms and become more popular under the influence of Christian carnival (Schauss 1938:269), but evidence suggests that Purim was a carnival celebration from the outset.

Festive laughter engendered by carnival has an intimate connection to changing seasons, "to the phases of the sun and moon, to the death and renewal of vegetation, and to the succession of agricultural seasons. In this succession all that is new or renews . . . is emphasized as a positive element [that] expresses the people's hopes of a happier future, of a more just social and economic order, of a new truth" (Bakhtin 1984b:81). In addition, the unique laughter of carnival is always directed toward something higher, such as the sun or other gods. Earthly authorities are ridiculed or killed, and the forms of carnival laughter are linked to death and rebirth (Bakhtin 1984a: 126-27). The Purim festival may have originally been a renewal or seasonal festival, and it certainly "expresses the people's hopes of a happier future, of a more just social and economic order." Seasonal festivals honor the natural rhythm of decay and rebirth, and the celebrations include such rituals as crowning and uncrowning, the burning of a winter effigy, and the consumption of harvested goods. While rites of passage affirm the changes in an individual's life, periodic festivals commemorate the continuity of the community.

Helmer Ringgren concludes that Purim is derived from a Persian New Year's ceremony,[11] but what clues suggest that Purim was originally some type of spring renewal or seasonal festival? The shared characteristics of Purim and various seasonal and New Year's festivals that Theodor Gaster (1950:12-13) has isolated are striking:

1. the celebration of a queen's selection and accession by holiday (= Esth 2:17-18)
2. the elevation and parading of a citizen in the clothes of a king (= Esth 6:1-11)
3. a fast (= Esth 4:15-16)
4. the execution of a malefactor (= Esth 7:10; 9:14, 25)
5. a battle between opposing parties (= Esth 9:1-17)
6. the distribution of gifts (= Esth 9:22)
7. a celebration around the time of the vernal equinox (= Esth 9:18-21)

Purim may, therefore, have originally been a non-Jewish spring renewal festival which the Jews adopted and modified, and the process may not have been unlike that used by the Christians who were influenced by pagan renewal rites and Roman Saturnalia.[12] Theodor Gaster hypothesizes about the development of these holidays within Christianity and Judaism:

> Purim may originally have been the Persian New Year festival held at the time of the vernal equinox and characterized by all the rites and ceremonies associated with that occasion in other parts of the ancient and modern worlds. When the Jews of Persia took it over, they did what people do everywhere in adapting borrowed institutions to their own need and outlooks. They fell back on a popular story which seemed to incorporate all the leading elements of the festival and proceeded to use it (with judicious alterations) as the explanation and justification of the festival's existence. It is in precisely the same way . . . that Easter and Yuletide became Christian festivals; and it is this process also which turned a primitive agricultural rite into the Israelite feast of Passover (1950:18).

One finds references in early Hebrew sources to a custom of "Purim leapings." Some interpreters have assumed that "leapings" is simply a synonym for "cavortings" and that the reference is to the general gaiety of the masquerades, but Gaster points out that these rites of leaping are common worldwide in connection with New Year or seasonal festivals (1950:67). The Purim festival of play, mischief, and wine-drinking may, therefore, have had the characteristic of a spring masquerade from its inception.

During the Middle Ages noise was a common element of Purim celebrations, but originally the beating and noise had nothing to do with Haman. They come from ancient times when Purim was a nature festival that commemorated the passing of winter and the approach of spring. The ancients believed evil spirits had great power to do mischief to all, especially when the seasons changed. Noisemaking became a safeguard against such spirits, and it survives in New Year's Eve celebrations today. The beating and noisemaking of Purim originally had this significance. It was only later, when Purim attained historic and religious significance, that the noisemaking was interpreted as the beating of Haman (Schauss 1938:265-66).

The election of a mock king, a popular feature of Purim celebrations and carnival, was also a custom in ancient societies. A member of the community would temporarily be established as monarch between the old year and the new. This rite was practiced in ancient Persia and Rome and may have also been practiced in Babylon (Gaster 1950:74).

As for the name of the Purim festival itself, the word is derived from *pur*, "lot," which does not exist in Hebrew or Aramaic, the languages spoken by the Jews at that time. The Babylonians believed that on New Year's Day the gods met and cast lots to determine the destinies of women and men for the next year. The process was understood as a type of "election day." Gaster (1950:8) mentions that the word "lot" may refer to the election of civic officers who were selected by this process. And finally, the idea that Purim was originally a Babylonian seasonal festival is also suggested by the names Mordecai and Esther, which are similar to the Babylonian male deity Marduk and female deity Ishtar. The parallel is reinforced by the fact that Mordecai and Esther are cousins, as are Ishtar and Marduk.

The Holiday's "Non-religious" Character

Carnival festivities and comic spectacle-rituals occupied an important place in the lives of people during the Middle Ages. These medieval carnival celebrations were "non-official" and unabashedly non-religious in nature:

> The basis of laughter which gives form to carnival rituals frees
> them completely from all religious and ecclesiastic dogmatism,
> from all mysticism and piety. They are also completely de-
> prived of the character of magic and prayer; they do not com-
> mand nor do they ask for anything. . . . All these forms are
> systematically placed outside . . . religiosity (Bakhtin 1984b: 7).

The evidence above suggests that the Esther tale may have originally been non-Jewish in origin. Purim may have once been a
pagan festival that was adopted and modified. Medieval carnival's non-religious character provides yet more evidence to support the view that the Hebrew version of the Esther narrative
was originally conceived within a carnivalesque framework.

The Hebrew version of the Esther narrative is part of a
much larger collection of books whereby almost nothing happens without the writer's reference to God's intervention and
instruction. But, as is often noted, God's name is never mentioned in the Esther (M) narrative. As Schauss puts it, "We get
the impression that the writer was somewhat afraid to mention
the name of God in [the] book" (1938:239). Schauss explains
that the author has incorporated material from "an old, heathen
festival" and has thereby decided that it would be distasteful to
include God and certain forms of religious practice in the
narrative. This view is popular.

> Although it purports to be a story of essentially Jewish inter-
> est, dealing with a situation affecting Jews and explaining the
> origin of a Jewish festival, every detail of its Jewish coloration
> involves something either anomalous or incredible. The Jewish
> hero and heroine—Mordecai and Esther—bear non-Jewish
> names. Mordecai is said to have been one of the persons
> originally deported from Jerusalem to Babylon—an identifica-
> tion which is chronologically grotesque, since the Babylonian
> Exile took place a full 112 years earlier. Esther is represented
> as the full consort of the Persian king; and this, in the light of
> known Persian usage, is no less bizarre (Gaster 1950:33).[13]

Bakhtin, whose sense of history is helpful, allows us to view
this "non-religious" dimension of the Hebrew Esther tale as part
of the literary carnivalesque. Indeed, the story's often mentioned non-religious character justifies our understanding of the
story as part of the carnivalesque from its inception.

Purim's Social Dimension

Another clue that Purim may have been a carnival celebration at the earliest stage lies in its social dimension. Those who assemble at the end of the story gather for a "cultic festal assembly," as the acts of violence and slaughter from the previous scenes move to the background and the festive celebrations move to the foreground (Clines 1984:161). This social event shall be observed "every year" and in "every generation," in "every family, province, and city" (9:26-28). Carnival celebrations such as this one described in the Esther (M) narrative recreate and renew the community. According to Esth 9:23, the Jews adopt this type of celebration "as a custom," and this corporate action of the people is then "reinforced and regularized" by Mordecai's letter (Fox 1991:119). Such carnival celebrations involve the individual in a community of participants and help the individual face the serious threats of life. The festival's treatment of death affirms life in a public setting through systematic, ritualized performances.

Bakhtin, in detailed analysis of the masquerading and buffoonery of carnival, suggests that such celebrating is specifically related to crisis situations: "Ritual laughter was a reaction to *crises* in the life of the sun (solstices), crises in the life of a deity, in the life of the world and of man (funeral laughter). In it, ridicule was fused with rejoicing" (1984a:127; original emphasis). Purim, a communal response to crisis, is carnivalesque at its core. The joy, which is evident in the celebration, is not just the community's release of high spirits in response to the resolution of crisis. It is also communally oriented. Purim is a day "for gladness and feasting," but also a holiday when "gifts of food [are sent] to one another" (9:19) and "presents [are given] to the poor" (9:22).[14] Mordecai subsequently records "these things" to ensure that the practice becomes a custom (9:20, 23).

Subverting the Status Quo

An additional shared characteristic exists between carnival and the earliest Purim celebrations. The celebration at the end of the story occurs because the man in power is overcome. Purim, like carnival celebrations in general, is about subverting the status quo. The Jews escape the genocidal wrath of an evil man and his idiotic superior and are thereby transformed in their historical condition.

Bakhtin studies ideological and descriptive aspects in an attempt to understand the opposition between the culture of officials and the culture of laughter as constants within the cultural history of humankind. The story of Esther is about dis-order, and the eruption of dis-order is part of the planned reading from the Esther scroll: "the Jewish masses understood both the scroll and the festival of Purim as being topsy-turvy" (Harris 1977:164). Specific verses are read in a louder voice than other verses, and hand held noisemakers are heard whenever the name of Haman is uttered. We observed in chapter 3 that the word *mishteh* ("banquet" or "feast") occurs as often in the book of Esther as elsewhere in the Hebrew Bible. The tendency toward drink reflected in the narrative itself has certainly become part of the traditional Purim celebration. Purim drinking is important because it leads to disorientation, which in turn leads to reversals, and the tradition of consuming enough drinks so that one is unable to distinguish between "Cursed be Haman" and "Blessed be Mordecai" is an element of the Purim festival that is rooted in the text.

Purim allows for deviations from the norm and sanctions what is otherwise not permitted: the wearing of clothes of the opposite sex, the burning of Haman's effigy, the eruption of noises, and so forth. These deviations and reversals underscore the switch in power: the once powerful Haman is brought low, and Esther, who along with the other virgins of the land is brought to the king's bedchamber, eventually rises to power and influence. The author indicates that the collective gaiety at the end of the story is brought about by a reversal: the fourteenth and fifteenth day of Adar are set aside "as the days on which the Jews gained relief from their enemies, and as *the month that had been turned for them* from sorrow into gladness and from mourning into a holiday," and the king "gave orders in writing that the wicked plot that [Haman] had devised against the Jews should come upon *his own* head, and that he and his sons should be hanged on the gallows" (9:22, 25; emphasis added). Haman's best laid plans produced the opposite result of his intended goal. And, of course, the collective gaiety at Purim is the ultimate subversion in this story. One man sets up a plan of mass genocide, but the intended victims celebrate at the end with "days of feasting and gladness" (9:22).

Conclusion

In sum, the collective gaiety at the end of the story has its own philosophical, aesthetic, and ideological essence, and a peculiar folk logic undergirds the cultural and literary life of this Hebrew narrative. The book belongs to the serio-comical genre, a tradition that reaches into the depths of the past. Rabelais's achievement was prepared for by centuries of development, and Bakhtin's description of carnival's language system has served as a lens through which to recover the virtually ignored idiom of carnival, so often obscure to us today. Indeed, a diminishing carnival perception of the world explains, in part, the futile efforts of interpreters who have expressed contempt for the narrative.

Both Rabelais and the author of the Esther narrative responded to official culture and dogma with carnivalized language, themes, and images. In the ancient Hebrew story— replete with clownish crownings and uncrownings, an official and non-official culture, lavish banquets, and the persistent fool—we witness a transposition of carnival into the language of literature. Renaissance carnival is the high point of a millennia-long development, and the Esther (M) tale is part, a very early part, of this historical process.

NOTES

BIBLIOGRAPHY

INDEXES

NOTES

NOTES TO CHAPTER 1
INTRODUCTION

[1] Because of this study's focus, the book most often quoted is *Rabelais and His World.* His other books are major contributions, and have, in fact, received more attention than *Rabelais and His World.* Cf. the section below, "Bakhtin's Major Works and the Bakhtin Circle."

[2] Though see Danna Nolan Fewell's comment: "One might also examine Esther in relation to the cultural (con)text of carnival . . . as it is so often played in modern Purim festivities" (1992:17). See also García-Treto's carnivalesque reading of 2 Kgs 9-10 (1992:153-71).

[3] Cf. esp. pp. 21, 22, 30, 42, 45, 76, 117, 148, 149, 230-32.

[4] With the exceptions of McCracken's book (1994) on the New Testament Gospels and the Greek *skandalon* and García-Treto's article (1992:153-71) on 2 Kgs 9-10. Scholars delivering papers at recent annual AAR/SBL meetings have drawn insight from Bakhtin: McCracken (1992) and Reed (1991).

[5] All three of these books have been translated into English: Medvedev/Bakhtin (1978); Voloshinov (1987); Voloshinov (1973).

[6] I. I. Kanaev, Lev Pumpiansky, Ivan Sollertinsky, Mikhail Tubyansky, Konstantin Vaghinov, and Maria Yudina.

[7] My research relies on critical translations of his work which are now readily available in the West.

[8] An excellent glossary of Bakhtin's technical vocabulary is included in Michael Holquist's edited version of *The Dialogic Imagination* (1981:423-434).

[9] These four articles are collected in the edited volume of *The Dialogic Imagination* (Bakhtin 1981). The third and fourth essays listed above are major works, totalling 175 and 164 pages respectively in the 1981 edition published by the University of Texas Press.

[10] The studies of Berg (1979), Clines (1984), Dommershausen (1968), and Fox (1991) are foremost in this regard.

[11] Many such important books have appeared in the last few years. Among them are: Bach (1990), Fewell and Gunn (1990), Loades (1990), Meyers (1988), and Trible (1978 and 1984).

[12] The story is set in the empire of Persia and Media (Esth 1:3,

14, 18, 19; 10:2), but abbreviated as Persia(n) in this study.

[13] Others could be mentioned as well, such as Josephus's paraphrase, Targum Sheni Aramaic, an Old Latin version, and a Proto-A text which predates the A-text.

[14] Michael Fox also treats these stories in a chapter titled "The Three Books of Esther" (1991:254-273) in his thorough study on character and ideology in Esther.

[15] Despite its strengths and refreshing tone—the NRSV has advanced us by light years—the new translation contains one glaring weakness: God is almost always portrayed with masculine terms ("he," "his"). At least one major hurdle remains. I have attempted elsewhere to suggest a few implications of the changes in translation made to the text of Jonah (from the RSV to the NRSV) where forty-seven of the forty-eight verses in the story have been altered (Craig 1993:19-44).

NOTES TO CHAPTER 2
THE LITERARY CARNIVALESQUE

[1] This topic is discussed in chap. 5.

[2] Mordecai may have some (limited) power at the palace. He is situated among the king's palace officials in 3:2-3, and Michael Fox points out that the conversation between Mordecai and the other officials appears to be among equals (1991:42). On the other hand, Esther is certainly powerless at the beginning of the story. She along with all "beautiful young virgins [are] sought out for the king" (2:2). They are "gathered together" (2:19) before they take turns going to the king in his bedchamber after a twelve month cosmetic treatment (2:12).

[3] Bakhtin 1984a:106-107; see also the glossary, pp. 305-22, for discussion of some of the proper names and works listed above.

[4] Bakhtin uses this term to refer to an author's single, dominating point of view reflected in a literary work. In contrast to the monologic novel, epitomized in Bakhtin's view by Dostoevsky, is the polyphonic novel: "A plurality of independent and unmerged voices and consciousnesses . . . of fully valid voices is in fact the chief characteristic of Dostoevsky's novels" (Bakhtin 1984a:6).

[5] Northrop Frye, in *Anatomy of Criticism*, includes Burton's *Anatomy of Melancholy* (1621) as a work following in the tradition of Menippus and Varro. Voltaire's *Candide* (1759) and Aldous Huxley's *Point Counter Point* (1928) are also characterized by menippean elements.

[6] LaCocque calls Esther the "most secular document of the Bible" (1990:83).

[7] See, for example, Esth 4:13-16 and 7:3-6.

NOTES TO CHAPTER 3
PRELUDE

1 Xerxes I, son of Darius, did indeed rule from India to Ethiopia (1:1). For discussions on Ahasuerus's identity, see Moore 1971:3-4 and Fox 1991:14-15.

2 Notice, for example, the interchange between Esther, Mordecai, and the king in 8:1-5. Mordecai and Esther stand in the king's presence *before* the "golden scepter" is extended. Cf. 4:11 and 5:2.

3 See 4:2, 11-14, 16b; 5:2; 8:4 and the next section.

4 See "The Laws" section later in this chapter.

5 The Persian empire never had more than thirty one satrapies (Moore 1971:4).

6 On these points see Clines 1984:219.

7 The biblical word *dat* ("law"), first used in the Persian period, appears twenty times in Esther (M): 1:8, 13, 15, 19; 2:8, 12; 3:8 (twice), 14, 15; 4:3, 8, 11, 16; 8:13, 14, 17; 9:1, 13, 14.

8 See Clines (1984:18-19) for significant comments on 8:8.

9 Esther explains this procedure herself: "Only if the king holds out the golden scepter to someone, may that person live" (4:11). Such amnesty is granted in 5:2 and in chap. 8, but notice the sequence of events (appearance before the king, then the scepter) in 8:3-4.

10 The secretaries of 3:12 are literally "the writers." They are simply the stenographers or copyists, and not the professional learned scribes mentioned, for example, in Jer 36:26.

11 This duplication is not found in Esther (A) or (B). The three words are found in 7:4, but the last two verbs are lacking in 3:13 (cf. Moore 1971:41). Thus the reversal, a distinguishing element in carnivalesque writings, is explicit in Esther (M) alone. The implications of reversals (or peripeties) in the book are discussed in chap. 4.

12 See the discussion on feasts in Rabelais's works in *Rabelais and His World* (Bakhtin 1984b:278-302).

13 According to Fox (1991:156, n. 4), *mishteh* occurs forty-six times in the Hebrew Bible, and twenty times in Esther.

14 Esther will prepare the next two banquets (5:4-8 and 7:1-9), and the Jews will celebrate with three feasts at the end (8:17; 9:17, 19; and 9:18).

15 The word is literally "a causing to rest." Translators understand "rest" differently: "holiday" (Vulgate and NRSV), "remission of taxes" (I Targum and RSV), "amnesty" (Greek). Cf. Moore 1971:25.

16 Conflicting perspectives on this and related issues are discussed in greater detail in chap. 6.

17 By contrast, Ahasuerus summons women for sex in the priva-

cy of his bedchamber, a room that is situated at the center of a concentric circle of power and authority: the "beautiful young virgins" (2:2) are brought *from* all the provinces *to* the harem *inside* the citadel of Susa. When her "turn" arrives, she *enters* the king's bedchamber and then returns *outside* to the harem the next morning (2:14).

[18] See Berg (1979:89, n. 67) and the sources she cites for possibilities about what the "king's gate" may denote.

[19] See Clines's (1984:34) excellent description of this information exchange.

[20] Josephus comments that "round his throne stood men with axes to punish any who approach the throne without being summoned" (Moore 1971:49).

NOTES TO CHAPTER 4
PERIPETY

[1] See especially, Berg 1979:104-113, 119 n. 42, Berg 1980: 115-19, Fox 1991:158-163, 243, 251-253, and LaCocque 1987:207.

[2] David Clines (1984:53) has called attention to Esther who, in 9:25, fades to the background: "The Hebrew makes no reference to Esther in v. 25: *uvevo'ah* must mean 'and when it (the matter) came (before the king)', since there is no mention of Esther in the context." By placing Esther in the background momentarily, the narrator accentuates Haman's plot against Mordecai which falls upon Haman's head. Notice also the emphasis on the hanging of Haman and his sons rather than the time of their hanging.

[3] Fox (1991:158-63) and Berg (1979:106-13) have discussed some of these parallels. I focus on the reversals in the brief discussion that follows.

[4] As Fox remarks, "The MT deliberately makes Esther pivotal in the transfer of Haman's property to Mordecai. . . . Esther acts freely. She could have retained control of Haman's estate for herself, for a Persian woman could hold wealth in her own right. . . . Esther is now a source of power and vast wealth" (1991:90-91).

[5] The reference to giving money is apparently to the money that Haman had volunteered to give in 3:9.

[6] The garment materials were mentioned in the description of opulent decorations during Ahasuerus's feast in the opening scene (1:6; Fox 1991:104).

[7] For a full discussion, see "The Grotesque Image of the Body and Its Sources" in Bakhtin 1984b:303-67.

[8] 1:9; cf. 1:1-8; 1:10-12.

[9] A few of the early rabbis concluded that Vashti was ordered to

appear naked before the crowd. They interpreted the phrase "wearing the royal crown" (1:11) to mean "wearing only the royal crown." See Fox 1991:165 and the sources he cites, b. Meg. 12b and Est. Rab. III 13-14.

[10] See Fox's comments on this topic (1991:33-34).

[11] This ambiguity arises because the narrator gives us only a partial view of Mordecai's mind at work, "Mordecai learned all that had been done" (4:1). No more than this is revealed.

[12] Mordecai is also described as wearing the fine linen (*buts*) of purple (*'arggaman*) in 8:15 that is reminiscent of the fine purple linen (*buts ve'arggaman*) of 1:6.

[13] The reference to someone other than the reigning monarch wearing the king's clothes has its parallel elsewhere in the Bible (Gen 41:38-42, 1 Sam 18:4, and 1 Kgs 1:33). Plutarch also tells of Teribazus's request for Artaxerxes II's robe in *Artaxerxes*, v (Moore 1971: 64-65). See also Berg 1979:62-64, 83 n. 9.

[14] The fact that Haman receives the ring sometime after the appointment as prime minister suggests that the gift was not given as a gesture when he was appointed.

[15] On the Gospel story's mock crowning and uncrowning of the "king of the Jews" and its impact on the literary carnivalesque, see Bakhtin 1984b:198. See also McCracken's book (1994).

[16] *Keter malekut* in 1:11; 2:17; 6:8; and *'ateret* in 8:15.

[17] Fox observes that Assyrian reliefs show kings' horses wearing crowns or pointed ornaments on their heads. These Assyrian reliefs suggest to him that the image of a crowned horse in Persia is "not out of the question" (Fox 1991:77). On the other hand, by removing one letter from the clause in Esth 6:8, the phrase may be translated as "[a horse] which the king has ridden while the royal diadem has been on his (the king's) head" (Clines 1984:192 n. 8).

[18] The use of *'atarah* ("headdress" or "crown") in 8:15 instead of *keter* ("crown") as before (1:11; 2:17; 6:8) appears to suggest that Mordecai does not receive the king's crown. But the significance of the scene should not be overlooked because Mordecai, like Esther and Vashti previously, does not ask for a crown, and the one he receives is "large" and "golden." As Clines remarks, if this is not the king's crown, it's "the next best thing to it" (1984:66). Moore understands the passage in a similar fashion. He cites 2 Sam 12:30 and suggests that the reference at Esth 8:15 is to a headdress different from the royal crown (1971:81).

[19] While biblical Hebrew does not have a neutral pronoun "it," it is obvious from the niphal construction of *katav* ("write") in 3:9 that

one should be supplied here when translating to English. Based on the context in which the word is used, it is clear that Haman does not ask Ahasuerus to do the writing.

20 The phrase "people or kindred" occurs, though in reverse order, in v. 20. Moore (1971:22) calls attention to the chiasm or crisscross pattern that is created by these words in vv. 10 and 20. They highlight the material that is found between the two verses.

21 The non-fiction massacres of Nazi Germany teach us that it only takes *one* nefarious man to set a pogrom in motion.

22 Moore (1971:19) agrees with Josephus, the Targums, and most commentators that these names are of well known ancient ancestors of Mordecai rather than his grandfather and great grandfather.

23 Haman, an Agagite, is mentioned in 3:1; 3:10; 8:3; 8:5; 9:24. In 3:1—Haman the son of Hammedatha the Agagite; 3:10—Haman the son of Hammedatha the Agagite, the enemy of the Jews; 8:3—Haman the Agagite; 8:5—Haman the son of Hammedatha the Agagite; 9:24—Haman son of Hammedatha the Agagite, the enemy of all the Jews.

24 Moore writes that, while racial or ethnic extraction may be distinct from religious affiliation, in the Hebrew Bible they are often "inseparably and inextricably bound up with one another in a mutually supportive relationship" (1971:37).

25 In contrast to this response, Esther is loquacious in her quoted speech before and after 7:6. In the Hebrew text, Esther speaks thirty three words in an uninterrupted fashion in 7:3-4, and in 8:5-6 she speaks forty seven words. By contrast, in 7:6 she utters only six words.

NOTES TO CHAPTER 5
PARODY

1 Except for chap. 10, which consists of only three verses and serves as a coda to the story.

2 See note 23 in chap. 4.

3 See the section, "Esther and Masks," in chap. 4 above

4 Cf. 3:4, the narrator's report of Haman's words to the king's servants. That Mordecai refuses to bow to Haman because of matters of faith is not made explicit, unlike the story of Daniel (3:1-18). See also the section, "Esther Reconsidered," in chap. 2 above.

5 The image of "standing" in 8:11 is important and probably intentional when we remember Haman's "falling" in 6:8.

6 8:13; 9:1, 5, 10, 16, 22.

7 A form of the word *herem*, which denotes "utter destruction"

at the time of holy war, is found in the passage that serves as background to the Agag-Saul tension (1 Sam 15:8, 9, 15, 18, 20), but the word is absent from Esth 9. The verb used in chap. 9 is *harag*, "kill" (9:10, 11, 12, 15, 16).

8 See, for example, the king's actions and words to Esther in 5:3, chap. 6, 7:2, 5-9, 8:1; also his words to Mordecai in chap. 6, 8:2, and to Esther and Mordecai in 8:7-8.

9 Humphreys (1985:98 and 149 n. 3) cites this quotation from Martin Luther's *Table Talk* xxiv.

10 Anderson 1950:42. After cataloguing disparaging viewpoints on the book of Esther (pp. 32-34), Anderson concludes with this comment: "Statements like these could easily be multiplied" (p. 34).

11 The enactment scene in chap. 9 contains no report of woman and children being killed.

12 Clines refers to the "hamfistedness" of chapters 9-10 (1984: 37), which is a "strange and questionable ending to the tale" (1984: 22), and concludes that the author of chaps. 9-10 is "no match for the practised author of the original tale" (1984:40). He finds that 9:1-9 is "defective" when compared to the preceding chapters, and he also points out that "many commentators" regard 9:20-32 or 9:20-10:3 "as secondary to the rest of the book" (1984:50). The commentators he mentions are Michaelis, Bertheau, Kamphausen, Wildeboer, and Paton. Clines acknowledges that more recent studies take the opposite view. Anderson, Bardtke, Gerleman, Moore, Dommershausen, and Berg express this more recent view.

13 This total is derived from the following verses: 500 in the fortress of Susa (9:6 and 9:12), the 10 sons of Haman (9:7 and 9:12), 300 in the city of Susa (9:15), and 75,000 in the provinces (9:16).

14 Literary wars do, of course, present problems. My point is not that chap. 9 *merely* reflects a literary war full of literary devices, but that it *is* a literary war.

15 The quotation is from Marilyn Stewart (1984:145), who quotes Rotsel's translation of Mikhail Bakhtin's *Problems of Dostoevsky's Poetics* (Ann Arbor, 1973).

16 Bakhtin uses the word "chronotope," literally "time-space," to refer to literary analysis based on the nature and ratio of temporal and spatial categories. In contrast to other theoreticians, he argues that the two categories are interdependent, and that neither category is privileged.

17 Berg writes that "some commentators think Ahasuerus exemplifies a capricious fool" (1979:63) and lists a number of sources to support the view (1979:84, n. 14). Cf. also the rabbinic sources that

Clines lists (1984:179, n. 3).

[18] The Hebrew word occurs only here and is notoriously difficult to translate. Moore suggests several possibilities (1971:25).

[19] Michael Fox (1991:81) cites three scholars, Talmon, Gerleman, and Dommershausen, who hold this view.

NOTES TO CHAPTER 6
PURIM

[1] See "Chapters 8-9 and the Literary Carnivalesque" and n. 12 in chap. 5 above.

[2] Bakhtin's concern with dialogue is evident in almost all of his writings. See esp. Bakhtin (1981), Medvedev/Bakhtin (1978), Voloshinov (1973).

[3] Though Bakhtin indicates that collective gaiety can only go so far in overcoming officialdom's oppressive structures in *The Dialogic Imagination*. Cf. also his comments about the Greek romances (1981: 60).

[4] Voltaire, for example, uses carnival forms in satire, but laughter is "reduced to bare mockery" (1984b:119). Elsewhere Bakhtin writes, "We have already described the fate of laughter in the eighteenth century: it loses its essential link with a universal outlook, it is combined with negation, and with a negation that is dogmatic" (1984b:101).

[5] Dommershausen (1968) has also expressed this view, though for different reasons than I am suggesting.

[6] Elsewhere in *Problems of Dostoevsky's Poetics* Bakhtin writes, "Laughter is a specific aesthetic relationship to reality, but not one that can be translated into logical language; that is, it is a specific means for artistically visualizing and comprehending reality and, consequently, a specific means for structuring an artistic image, plot, or genre" (1984a:164).

[7] Bakhtin views collective gaiety as victory over fear: "It was the victory of laughter over fear that most impressed medieval man [and woman]. . . . It was the defeat of . . . authoritarian commandments and prohibitions. . . . Through this victory laughter clarified [our] consciousness and gave [us] a new outlook on life. This truth was ephemeral; it was followed by the fears and oppressions of everyday life, but from these brief moments another unofficial truth emerged, truth about the world . . . which prepared the new Renaissance consciousness. The acute awareness of victory over fear is an essential element of medieval laughter" (1984b:90-91).

[8] These five scrolls are printed together within the Writings (*Ketuvim*) in most editions of the Hebrew Bible.

⁹ The custom of celebrating the anniversary of different escapes from danger eventually became international communal events. The reason for these observances are varied, and an extensive list of special Purims is found in Shmeruk 1971:1395-1400.

¹⁰ I am indebted to Gaster (1950:59-78), Harris (1977:164-67), Jacobs (1971:1390-95), Schauss (1938:258), and Shmeruk (1971: 1396-1404) in the discussion that follows.

¹¹ Moore (1971:xlviii). In a more moderate tone, Moore concludes that a Persian origin is "probable but not provable" (1971:xlix).

¹² Moore (1971:xlix, n. 71) writes, "According to Bede . . . our English word 'Easter' goes back to Ostara, the Teutonic goddess of spring; and as is well known, the pagan Roman Saturnalia, celebrated December 19-25, had certain customs and attitudes not incompatible with Christmas."

¹³ Gaster concludes that the Hebrew narrative is an adaptation of a popular Persian novella (1950:35). In the introductory article on Esther in the NRSV, the author refers to what was "probably" the tale's pagan festival base (NRSV:612 [OT]). Commenting on the book's popularity, Schauss observes that Purim is the only Jewish holiday "not imbued with religious solemnity." The holiday lacks religious observances or ceremonials, and practically all the customs originated from "heathen observances" (1938:254, 264).

¹⁴ The custom of sending portions (*manot*) is also attested at Neh 8:10, 12.

BIBLIOGRAPHY

Allis, Oswald T. 1923. "The Reward of the King's Favorite (Esther vi. 8)." *The Princeton Theological Review* 21:621-32.

Anderson, Bernhard W. 1950. "The Place of the Book of Esther in the Christian Bible." *Journal of Religion* 30:32-43.

Andrew, M. E. 1975. "Esther, Exodus, and Peoples." *Australian Biblical Review* 23:25-28.

Bach, Alice, ed. 1990. *The Pleasure of Her Text: Feminist Readings of Biblical and Historical Texts*. Philadelphia: Trinity Press International.

Bakhtin, Mikhail. 1981. *The Dialogic Imagination*. Trans. Caryl Emerson and Michael T. Holquist. Austin: University of Texas.

———. 1984a. *Problems of Dostoevsky's Poetics*. Trans. Caryl Emerson. Minneapolis: University of Minnesota.

———. 1984b. *Rabelais and His World*. Trans. Hélène Iswolsky. Bloomington: Indiana University.

Ballmann, E. A. 1967. "Esther, Book of." *New Catholic Encyclopedia* 5:556-57.

Bardtke, Hans. 1963. *Das Buch Esther*. KAT XVII 5. Gütersloh.

Baumgarten, A. I. 1971. "Scroll of Esther." *Encyclopaedia Judaica* 14:1047-57.

Ben-Yosef, Arie. 1985. "*Lekah Tov*—The First Book Printed in Eretz-Israel and its Author." *Hebrew Studies* 26:319-23.

Berg, Sandra Beth. 1979. *The Book of Esther: Motifs, Themes and Structure*. SBLDS 44. Missoula: Scholars.

———. 1980. "After the Exile: God and History in the Books of Chronicles and Esther." In *The Divine Helmsman*. James L. Crenshaw and Samuel Sandmel, eds. New York: Ktav. Pp. 107-27.

Bergey, Ron. 1984. "Late Linguistic Features in Esther." *Jewish Quarterly Review* 17:66-78.

Bickerman, Elias. 1967. *Four Strange Books of the Bible: Jonah, Daniel, Koheleth, Esther*. New York: Schocken.

Bos, Johanna W. H. 1986. *Ruth, Esther, Jonah*. Atlanta: John Knox.

Carroll, David. 1983. "The Alterity of Discourse: Form, History, and the Question of the Political in M. M. Bakhtin." *Diacritics* 13:65-83.

Carroll, Michael P. 1983. "Myth, Methodology, and Transformation in the Old Testament: The Stories of Esther, Judith, and Susanna." *Studies in Religion* 12:301-12.

Cazelles, Henri. 1961. "Note sur la composition du rouleau d'Esther."

In *Lex tua veritas: Festschrift für Hubert Junker*. H. Gross and F. Mussner, eds. Trier: Paulinus. Pp. 17-29.

Clark, Katerina and Michael T. Holquist. 1984. *Mikhail Bakhtin*. Cambridge: Harvard University.

Clines, David J. A. 1984. *The Esther Scroll: The Story of the Story*, JSOTS 30. Sheffield: JSOT.

——. 1990. "Reading Esther from Left to Right." In *The Bible in Three Dimensions*. JSOTS 87. David J. A. Clines, Stephen E. Fowl, and Stanley E. Porter, eds. Sheffield: Sheffield Academic. Pp. 31-52.

Coggins, Richard J. and S. Paul Re'emi. 1985. *Israel among the Nations: A Commentary on the Books of Nahum and Obadiah*, International Theological Commentary. Grand Rapids: Eerdmans.

Cohen, Abraham. D. 1974. "'Hu ha-goral': The Religious Significance of Esther." *Judaism* 23:87-94.

Costas, Orlando E. 1988. "The Subversiveness of Faith: Esther as a Paradigm for a Liberating Theology." *The Ecumenical Review* 40: 66-78.

Craghan, John. 1982a. "Esther, Judith, and Ruth, Paradigms for Human Liberation." *Biblical Theology Bulletin* 12:11-19.

——. 1982b. *Esther, Judith, Tobit, Jonah, Ruth*. OT Message 16. Wilmington, DE: Michael Glazier.

Craig, Kenneth M. 1993. *A Poetics of Jonah: Art in the Service of Ideology*. Columbia: University of South Carolina.

Crenshaw, J. L. 1969. "Method in Determining Wisdom Influence upon 'Historical' Literature." *Journal of Biblical Literature* 88: 129-42.

Daube, D. 1946-1947. "The Last Chapter of Esther." *Jewish Quarterly Review* 37:139-47.

Dommershausen, Werner. 1968. *Die Estherrolle*. Stuttgarter Biblische Monographien 6. Stuttgart: Katholisches Bibelwerk.

Driver, G. R. 1954. "Problems and Solutions." *Vetus Testamentum* 4:225-45.

Eagleton, Terry. 1983. *Literary Theory: An Introduction*. Minneapolis: University of Minnesota.

Fewell, Danna Nolan. 1992. "Introduction: Writing, Reading, and Relating." In *Reading Between Texts: Intertextuality and the Hebrew Bible*. Danna Nolan Fewell, ed. LCBI. Louisville: Westminster/John Knox. Pp. 11-20.

Fewell, Danna Nolan and David Miller Gunn. 1990. *Compromising Redemption: Relating Characters in the Book of Ruth*. LCBI. Louisville: Westminster/John Knox.

Fiorenza, Elisabeth Schüssler. 1984. *In Memory of Her: A Feminist Theological Reconstruction of Christian Origins*. New York: Crossroads.

Fisch, Harold. 1988. *Poetry with a Purpose: Biblical Poetics and Interpretation*. Bloomington and Indianapolis: Indiana University.

Fox, Michael V. 1991. *Character and Ideology in the Book of Esther.* Columbia: University of South Carolina.

Fredman, Norman J. 1976. "Themes in the Book of Esther." *Dor le Dor* 5:111-23.

Freedman, H. and Maurice Simon, eds. 1951. *Midrash Rabbah: Esther and Song of Songs.* Trans. Maurice Simon. London: Soncino.

Gan, Moshe. 1961-1962. "The Book of Esther in the Light of the Story of Joseph in Egypt" (Hebrew). *Tarbiz* 31:144-49.

García-Treto, Francisco O. 1992. "The Fall of the House: A Carnivalesque Reading of 2 Kings 9 and 10." In Danna Nolan Fewell, ed., *Reading Between Texts: Intertextuality and the Hebrew Bible.* LCBI. Louisville: Westminster/John Knox Press. Pp. 153-71.

Gardner, Anne E. 1984. "The Relationship of the Additions to the Book of Esther to the Maccabean Crisis." *Journal for the Study of Judaism in the Persian, Hellenistic, and Roman Period* 15:1-8.

Gaster, Theodor H. 1950. *Purim and Hanukkah in Custom and Tradition.* New York: Henry Schuman.

Gehman, Henry S. 1924. "Notes on the Persian Words in the Book of Esther." *Journal of Biblical Literature* 43:321-28.

Gerleman, Gillis. 1968. "Studien zu Esther." *Biblische Studien* 48:1-48.

Goldman, Stan. 1990. "Narrative and Ethical Ironies in Esther." *Journal for the Study of the Old Testament* 47:15-31.

Gordis, Robert. 1972. *Megillat Esther: The Masoretic Hebrew Text with Introduction, New Translation and Commentary.* New York: The Rabbinical Assembly.

——. 1976. "Studies in the Esther Narrative." *Journal of Biblical Literature* 95:43-58.

——. 1981. "Religion, Wisdom and History in the Book of Esther—a New Solution to an Ancient Crux." *Journal of Biblical Literature* 100:359-88.

Grasham, W. W. 1973. "The Theology of the Book of Esther." *Restoration Quarterly* 16:99-111.

Greenblatt, Stephen J., ed. 1981. *Allegory and Representation.* Baltimore: The Johns Hopkins Press.

Greenstein, Edward L. 1987. "A Jewish Reading of Esther." In *Judaic Perspectives on Ancient Israel.* Jacob Neusner, ed. Philadelphia: Fortress. Pp. 225-43.

Gunn, David M. and Danna Nolan Fewell. 1993. *Narrative in the Hebrew Bible.* London and New York: Oxford University.

Hallo, William W. 1983. "The First Purim." *Biblical Archaeologist* 46:19-27.

Hambrick-Stowe, Charles E. 1983. "Ruth the New Abraham, Esther the New Moses." *Christian Century* 100:1130-34.

Harris, Monford. 1977. "Purim: The Celebration of Dis-Order." *Judaism* 26:161-70.

Harvey, Dorothea. 1962a. "Esther, Book of." In *The Interpreter's*

Dictionary of the Bible, 2. George A. Buttrick, ed. Nashville: Abingdon. Pp. 149-51.

——. 1962b. "Vashti." In *The Interpreter's Dictionary of the Bible*, 4. George A. Buttrick, ed. Nashville: Abingdon. Pp. 746-74.

Haupt, Paul. 1908. "Critical Notes on Esther." *American Journal of Semitic Languages and Literature* 24:97-186.

Herst, Roger E. 1973. "The Purim Connection." *Union Seminary Quarterly Review* 28:139-45.

Horn, Siegfried H. 1964. "Mordecai, a Historical Problem." *Biblical Research* 9:14-25.

Humphreys, W. Lee. 1973. "A Life-Style for Diaspora: A Study of the Tales of Esther and Daniel." *Journal of Biblical Literature* 92: 211-23.

——. 1976. "Esther, Book of." In *Interpreter's Dictionary of the Bible Supplement*. Nashville: Abingdon. Pp. 279-81.

——. 1985. "The Story of Esther and Mordecai: An Early Jewish Novella." In *Saga, Legend, Tale, Novella, Fable*. George W. Coats, ed. JSOTS 35. Sheffield: Sheffield Academic. Pp. 97-113.

Hyman, Frieda Clark. 1986. "The Education of a Queen." *Judaism* 35:78-85.

Jackson, Richard. 1987. "The Dialogic Self." *Georgia Review* 41: 415-20.

Jacobs, Louis. 1971. "Purim." *Encyclopaedia Judaica* 13:1390-95.

Jones, Bruce William. 1977. "Two Misconceptions about the Book of Esther." *Catholic Biblical Quarterly* 39:171-81.

——. 1978. "The So-Called Appendix to the book of Esther." *Semitics* 6:36-43.

Kilmer, Anne Draffkorn. 1991. "An Oration on Babylon." *Altorientalische Forschungen* 18:9-22.

Knight, George A. F. 1955. *Esther, Song of Songs, Lamentations*. London: SCM.

Lachs, Samuel T. 1979. "Hadassah that is Esther." *Journal for the Study of Judaism in the Persian, Hellenistic, and Roman Period* 10:219-20.

LaCocque, André. 1987. "Haman in the Book of Esther." *Hebrew Annual Review* 11:207-22.

——. 1990. *The Feminine Unconventional: Four Subversive Figures in Israel's Tradition*. Minneapolis: Fortress.

Lebram, J. C. H. 1972. "Purimfest und Estherbuch." *Vetus Testamentum* 22:208-22.

Levenson, Jon D. 1976. "The Scroll of Esther in Ecumenical Perspective." *Journal of Ecumenical Studies* 13:440-52.

Lewy, Julius. 1939. "The Feast of the 14th Day of Adar." *Hebrew Union College Annual* 14:127-51.

Littmann, Robert J. 1974. "The Religious Policy of Xerxes and the Book of Esther." *Jewish Quarterly Review* 65:145-55.

Loader, J. A. 1978. "Esther as a Novel with Different Levels of Meaning." *Zeitschrift für die alttestamentliche Wissenschaft* 90:417-21.

Loades, Ann, ed. *Feminist Theology: A Reader*. 1990. Louisville: Westminster/John Knox.

Loewenstamm, Samuel E. 1971. "Esther 9:29-32: The Genesis of a Late Edition." *Hebrew Union College Annual* 42:117-24.

Magonet, Jonathan. 1980. "The Liberal and the Lady: Esther Revisited." *Judaism* 29:167-76.

Mayer, Rudolf. 1961. "Iranischer Beitrag zu Problemen des Daniel und Esther-Buches." In *Lex tua veritas: Festschrift für Hubert Junker*. H. Gross and F. Mussner, eds. Trier: Paulinus. Pp. 127-35.

McCracken, David. 1992. "Character in the Boundary: Bakhtin's Interdividuality in Biblical Narratives." Paper delivered on 22 November 1992 at the Society of Biblical Literature Annual Meeting, San Francisco.

——. 1994. *The Scandal of the Gospels: Jesus, Story, and Offense*. London and New York: Oxford University.

McKane, W. 1961. "A Note on Esther IX and 1 Samuel XV." *Journal of Theological Studies* 12:260-61.

Medvedev, P. N./M. M. Bakhtin. 1978. *The Formal Method in Literary Scholarship: A Critical Introduction to Sociological Poetics*. Baltimore: Johns Hopkins University.

Meinhold, Arndt. 1976. "Die Gattung der Josephgeschichte und des Estherbuches: Diasporanovelle II." *Zeitschrift für die alttestamentliche Wissenschaft* 88:72-93.

Meyers, Carol. 1988. *Discovering Eve: Ancient Israelite Women in Context*. London and New York: Oxford University.

Millard, A. R. 1977. "The Persian Names in Esther and the Reliability of the Hebrew Text." *Journal of Biblical Literature* 96:481-88.

Miller, Charles H. 1980. "Esther's Levels of Meaning." *Zeitschrift für die alttestamentliche Wissenschaft* 92:145-48.

Montefiore, C. G. 1899. *The Bible for Home Reading*. Vol. 2. New York: The Macmillan Company.

Moore, Carey A. 1971. *Esther*. Anchor Bible. Garden City: Doubleday.

——. 1975. "Archaeology and the Book of Esther." *Biblical Archaeologist* 38:62-79.

——. 1977. *Daniel, Esther, and Jeremiah: The Additions*. Anchor Bible. Garden City: Doubleday.

——, ed. 1982. *Studies in the Book of Esther*. New York: Ktav.

——. 1983. "Esther Revisited Again: A Further Examination of Certain Esther Studies of the Past Ten Years." *Hebrew Annual Review* 7:169-86.

——. 1985. "Esther Revisited: An Examination of Esther Studies over the Past Decade." In *Biblical and Related Studies Presented to Samuel Iwry*. Ann Kort and Scott Morschauser, ed. Winona Lake: Eisenbrauns. Pp. 163-72.

——. 1987. "Eight Questions Most Frequently Asked about the Book of Esther." *Bible Review* 3:16-31.

——. 1992. "Esther, Book of." In *The Anchor Bible Dictionary*. Vol. 2. David Noel Freedman, eds. New York: Doubleday. Pp. 633-43.

Morris, A. E. 1930-1931. "The Purpose of the Book of Esther." *Expository Times* 42:124-28.

Niditch, Susan. 1985. "Legends of Wise Heroes and Heroines." In *The Hebrew Bible and Its Modern Interpreters*. Douglas A. Knight and Gene M. Tucker, eds. Philadelphia/Chico: Fortress/Scholars. Pp. 445-63.

Niditch, Susan and Robert Doran. 1977. "The Success Story of the Wise Courtier: A Formal Approach." *Journal of Biblical Literature* 96:179-93.

Oppenheim, A. Leo. 1965. "On Royal Gardens in Mesopotamia." *Journal of Near Eastern Studies* 24:328-33.

Paton, Lewis B. 1908. *A Critical and Exegetical Commentary on the Book of Esther*. ICC. New York: Scribner.

Penchansky, David. 1990. *The Betrayal of God: Ideological Conflict in Job*. LCBI. Louisville, KY: Westminster/John Knox.

Polzin, Robert. 1984. "Dialogic Imagination in the Book of Deuteronomy." *Studies in Twentieth Century Literature* 9:135-43.

——. 1989. *Samuel and the Deuteronomist: A Literary Study of the Deuteronomic History*. San Francisco: Harper & Row.

Pomorska, Krystyna. 1978. "Mixail Baxtin and His Verbal Universe." *PTL: A Journal for Descriptive Poetics and Theory of Literature* 3:379-86.

Porten, Bezalel. 1971a. "Haman." *Encyclopaedia Judaica* 7:1222-24.

——. 1971b. "Mordecai." *Encyclopaedia Judaica* 12:307-309.

Rabelais, François. 1936 edition. *Gargantua and Pantagruel*. Trans. Jacques LeClercq. New York: The Modern Library.

Raskin, Marina. 1981. "Review of *The Dialogic Imagination*." *Modern Fiction Studies* 27:667-69.

Reed, Walter. 1991. "The Bible According to Mikhail Bakhtin: A Dialogics of Scripture." Paper delivered on 24 November 1991 at the Society of Biblical Literature Annual Meeting, Kansas City.

Rosenberg, Joel. 1975. "Meanings, Morals, and Mysteries: Literary Approaches to Torah." *Response* 9:67-94.

Rosenthal, Ludwig A. 1895. "Die Josephgeschichte, mit den Büchern Ester und Daniel verglichen." *Zeitschrift für die alttestamentliche Wissenschaft* 15:278-84.

Ruether, Rosemary Radford. 1983. *Sexism and God-Talk: Toward a Feminist Theology*. Boston: Beacon.

Rylaarsdam, J. C. 1962. "Purim." In *The Interpreter's Dictionary of the Bible*, 3. George A. Buttrick, ed. Nashville: Abingdon. Pp. 968-69.

Sasson, Jack M. 1987. "Esther." In *The Literary Guide to the Bible*. Robert Alter and Frank Kermode, eds. Cambridge: Harvard

University. Pp. 335-42.

Schauss, Hayyim. 1938. *The Jewish Festivals*. Trans. Samuel Jaffe. Cincinnati: Union of American Hebrew Congregations.

Shea, William H. 1976. "Esther and History." *Andrews University Seminary Studies* 14:227-46.

Shmeruk, Chone. 1971. "Purim-shpil." *Encyclopaedia Judaica* 13: 1396-1404.

Siegel, Monique R. 1985. "Book of Esther—A Novelle." *Dor le Dor* 14:142-51.

Sterk, Jan P. 1985. "How Many Books of Esther are There?" *The Bible Translator* 36:440-42.

Stewart, Marilyn. 1984. "Carnival and *Don Quixote*: The Folk Tradition of Comedy." In Louise Cowan, ed., *The Terrain of Comedy*. Dallas: The Dallas Institute of Humanities and Culture. Pp. 143-62.

Sturrock, John. 1986. "Jamboree." *London Review of Books* 8:13-14.

Talmon, S. 1963. "'Wisdom' in the Book of Esther." *Vetus Testamentum* 13:419-55.

Thornton, T. C. G. 1986. "The Crucifixion of Haman and the Scandal of the Cross." *Journal of Theological Studies* 37:419-26.

Todorov, Tzvetan. 1981. *Mikhail Bakhtin. Le principe dialogique*. Paris: Éditions du Seuil.

Torrey, Charles C. 1944. "The Older Book of Esther." *Harvard Theological Review* 37:1-40.

Tov, Emanuel. 1982. "The 'Lucianic' Text of the Canonical and the Apocryphal Sections of Esther: A Rewritten Biblical Book." *Textus* 10:1-25.

Trible, Phyllis. 1978. *God and the Rhetoric of Sexuality*. Philadelphia: Fortress.

——. 1984. *Texts of Terror: Literary-Feminist Readings of Biblical Narrative*. Minneapolis: Augsburg Fortress.

Voloshinov, V. N. 1973. *Marxism and the Philosophy of Language*. New York: Seminar.

——. 1987. *Freudianism: A Critical Sketch*. Bloomington: Indiana University.

White, Sidnie Ann. 1992. "Esther." In *The Women's Bible Commentary*. Carol A. Newsom and Sharon H. Ringe, eds. Louisville: Westminster/John Knox. Pp. 124-29.

Wright, J. Stafford. 1970. "The Historicity of the Book of Esther." In *New Perspectives on the Old Testament*. J. Barton Payne, ed. Waco: Word Books. Pp. 37-47.

Zadok, Ran. 1986. "Notes on Esther." *Zeitschrift für die alttestamentliche Wissenschaft* 98:105-10.

Zeitlin, Solomon. 1972. "The Books of Esther and Judith: A Parallel." In *The Book of Judith*. Jewish Apocryphal Literature, vol. 7. Morton S. Enslin, ed. Leiden: E. J. Brill. Pp. 1-37.

INDEXES

AUTHORS

BIBLICAL REFERENCES